Mindfulness-Based Counseling

For

Self-Regulation

Dale Starcher, PhD

ISBN: 1439271801
ISBN-13: 9781439271803

Acknowledgement:

There have been a number of colleagues and friends who provided helpful advice as I developed these treatment protocols. They include: Charles Williams, George Colnaghi, Frank Haronian, Les Fehmi, Rob Kall, John Myers, and Theodore Toscano. Thank you.

Preface

Purpose of this Training Manual

Guides the therapist in using mindfulness-based strategies related to relaxation, therapeutic imagery, and biofeedback with adolescents and adults

Demonstrates how these three broad approaches can be seamlessly integrated into a program of stress reduction and self-regulation

Provides the therapist with a step-by-step training program

Offers an introductory, yet comprehensive program

Makes it as easy as possible for the therapist to import these approaches into his or her existing therapy program.

Current research on mental health has focused in an almost dramatic way on the significance of stress. For example, with many of the most severe disorders, such as psychosis, attachment disorder, and borderline personality disorder, the "stress-vulnerability model" is often used to explain how symptoms can increase under stress. One reason that stress has become an important construct is because it represents a view of health that includes both mind and body. The health care field has finally recognized the need to integrate mind and body into a single conception in the way we view, as well as address, mental health issues.

In terms of treatment approaches, much emphasis is being placed these days on the use of mindfulness-based self-regulation models. Self-regulation is typically viewed from a cognitive behavioral perspective. Like the stress construct, self-regulation is also an integrative perspective, where the term may apply to either mind or body, or both.

While the thrust of this training manual is based on the view that mind and body can be self-regulated, if you study the history of psychology, you will find a schism between the mind and body. From the late 1800s until more recently, the role of body in psychotherapy had been ignored from any serious study by the majority of investigators. As a result of this schism, psychotherapists have failed to utilize the highly significant role that the body plays in the psychotherapy process until more recently.

Over the last 20 to 40 years, there have been excellent investigations and thousands of research studies on mind-body phenomena: Investigators such as Hans Selye, the physician who originated the concept called "stress" and published over 1500 research papers describing the role of stress in illness; and Milton Erickson, whose theories and procedures revolutionized hypnotherapy and recognized how the body played an essential role in any healing. Selye, Erickson, and other investigators (e.g., Bernheim, Jacobson, Wiener, Meyers & Sperry, Schultz & Luthe, Benson, Green & Green, Schwartz, Hilgard, Gazzaniga, and Rossi) have brought new ideas which are impacting the entire field of health care, enabling mind and body to be brought back together again for the purpose of healing and growth.

The overall impact of these investigations has been so revolutionary that an entirely new field of health care has arisen to bridge this schism between mind and body. This field is referred to by different names: Behavioral medicine, health psychology, applied psychophysiology, etc. The result is a tremendous advancement in our understanding from which all health care professionals can benefit. For the therapist it brings, not only new methods and techniques, but also a larger conceptualization of psychological processes, leading to new insights in the healing process.

Let us start from the conceptualization that mind and body are two subsystems of one system. It can help to think of this system as an information system, where information from one subsystem is transformed to the other subsystem. Support for this kind of interaction comes from many sources. For example, Green, Green, and Walters (1979) state: Every change in the physiological state is accompanied by an appropriate change in the mental-emotional state, conscious or subconscious and, conversely, every change in the mental-emotional state, conscious or subconscious, is accompanied by an appropriate change in the physiological state (p. 132). While it may be convenient to think at times of the body and mind as being two subsystems we should not forget that both are always somehow involved in the psychotherapy process.

People are aware of their body through their central nervous system, meaning that experience of body is a psychological experience (Green, et al, 1986). All we are doing when we take a mind-body perspective is rightfully including biology as part of any and all psychological experiences. Any experience at the physiological level is automatically experienced at the psychological level, and vice versa. To ignore physiology in counseling is, in actuality, to ignore a part of mind and personality. By adding this new and expanded perspective, the therapist can be more effective in the use of treatment strategies. This will become more and more clear as you work your way through the manual.

The ability to consciously regulate what was previously involuntary or subconscious processes is well documented in the literature. This training manual will discuss the theories supporting self-regulation, its benefits in therapy, and the kinds of therapeutic strategies that are particularly helpful in attaining conscious self-regulation. There are essentially two ways that you, the therapist, can benefit from this new knowledge: First, by understanding the role of mind-body self-regulation within the context of therapy and, second, by re-conceptualizing counseling so that new insights can arise on ways that will help you enhance the healing process.

There are different theoretical perspectives that one may take in incorporating these new approaches. However, rather than espousing a single theoretical framework, this manual starts with the premise that a synthesis of theoretical perspectives is more helpful. This larger context is used, for example, when addressing symptoms, underlying dynamics, positive psychology, and self-actualization. Here, we move away theoretically from a strictly behavioral, cognitive, psychodynamic, or humanistic view. Symptoms and personality dynamics, cognitions and body, can all be addressed as needed to elicit change.

Let me add that the uniqueness of each therapist will vary in the manner in which this integration and progression occurs. While we need to be logical and systematic when it is practical to do so, therapy is, to a large extent, an intuitive and creative process, lending itself to individual differences, particularly because each client is unique. All that matters is that the therapist must inevitably measure his or her effectiveness by whether the client has achieved the needed changes.

Dale Starcher

Table of Contents

Chapter 6: Therapeutic Imagery Training

Chapter 7: The Heart of Emotions:

Chapter 8: Teaching Beginning Meditation:

About the Author

I

Brief Review

Purpose of this Chapter

**A brief review of the foundation on which current
mindfulness-based strategies have been built**

**Discussion of some of the approaches that are
currently being used**

**How these approaches can be integrated within
a treatment program**

How Current Methods Came into Practice

The oldest records of cultures practicing mindfulness-based stress reduction, self-reflection strategies, and self-regulation methods are from India, which has enjoyed a long tradition over thousands of years. There are, for example, sculptures dating back as much as 5,000 years depicting yoga stretches and meditation postures.

The term "mindulfulness" is especially found in Buddhism and has to do with our ability to observe our mind's thoughts and emotions, as well be more observant and less reactive of others' responses toward us. This leads to a number of benefits, such as our ability to stop habitual responses, develop greater clarity related to the source of our thoughts and feelings, be less reactive to other people, and enable us to make more conscious and adaptive responses.

In Western culture, we do not find much interest in these kinds of strategies until much more recently. In the mid 1800s, for instance, the Romantic Movement in Europe was quite popular and included much interest in Asian teachings like meditation. This period also saw the birth of what eventually become the fields of psychology and psychotherapy, as well as mind-body medicine, a resurgent interest in herbal treatments, along with health spas and other body therapies.

A second resurgence took place in the West in the late 1950's with the birth of the cognitive neurosciences. This was significant because it made the focus on the mind respectable again following the domination of behaviorism. This was quickly followed in the 1960s with the development of electronic and computer based instruments for measuring mind, brain, and bodily processes here-to-fore beyond our grasp. This soon led to the use of biofeedback and the development of research based relaxation techniques, body therapies, etc. This movement has continued through the present time.

Meditation and Yoga

In Asia, where no philosophical schism has existed between the mind and body, relaxation, meditation and other self-regulation methods have played a central role in the traditional and folk healing arts over the last four thousand years. Traditional *ayurvedic* medicine, as well as the yogis, monks, sufis, and folk physicians knew the power of mind-body self-regulation, particularly in accessing the subconscious and in re-balancing the mind-body system. Their own control over mind-body processes have been well documented by Western scientists, mostly through the use of sophisticated biofeedback instrumentation.

It's quite amazing that very sophisticated self-regulation methods were developed thousands of years ago in Asia.

One wide spread use of meditation in the West is the technique called Transcendental Meditation, which has been well researched by Herbert Benson and used in the development of his own treatment approach, the "Relaxation Response" (Benson, 1975). This is essentially the use of a sound syllable or word, called a *mantra* that is repeated silently to oneself for at least 20 minutes. Besides psychological affects, the Relaxation Response has also been shown clinically to lower blood pressure

Another popular import from Asia is the use of *Hatha* Yoga across therapeutic settings, gyms, and spas, etc. *Hatha* Yoga consists mainly of specially designed stretching and breathing exercises. This form of yoga is used for relaxing and strengthening the neuromuscular system, energizing the entire body, and strengthening and maintaining a more flexible spinal column. Some also claim that *Hatha* Yoga can even help balance and energize the endocrine glands (Vishnudevananda, 1959; Bhatnagar, 1980).

Autogenic Training

In the West, the early 1900's brought a focus of the mind-body issue to the health care field. In the 1920's, Johannes Schultz, a German psychiatrist and neurologist, had become familiar with earlier German studies on self-hypnosis. From these and his own research, as well as his research of Indian Yoga, he developed the technique Autogenic Training, where the term "autogenic" means "self-generating." His goal was to develop a method that could be initiated and practiced by the client, accessing his or her own inner resources for self-healing. This goal strives to access "homeostatic self-regulatory brain mechanisms" (Luthe, 1979). Luthe and others' extensive research on Autogenic Training has clearly demonstrated it's ability to help regain homeostatic balances in the treatment of many organic, psychosomatic, and psychiatric disorders.

Progressive Relaxation

In the U.S. around the same time period as the development of Autogenic Training, Jacobson, a physician at Yale Medical School, developed his own mind-body method of healing called Progressive Relaxation (PR, also called Progressive Muscle Relaxation), where he researched the effects of relaxation of the neuromuscular system. In his effort to objectively measure muscle tension, he elicited the expertise of Bell Laboratories. The result was the development of the first electromyograph (EMG). This medical instrument was extremely helpful in validating Jacobson's theories on muscle tension and its relation to functional disorders. Extensive research by Jacobson (1934) and others have shown PR to be effective in healing a variety of organic, psychosomatic and psychiatric disorders. Like Autogenic Training, PR uses the client's own inner self-regulatory forces for healing, helping to resolve previous imbalances in the mind-body system.

Jacobson was a pioneer in the field of applied psychophysiology and can be credited with giving scientific recognition in this country to the importance of relaxation training for physical and psychological disorders, as well as in the development of the EMG, which eventually led to its use as a valuable instrument for medical evaluation and as a biofeedback modality. Autogenic Training, Progressive Muscle Relaxation, and Transcendental Meditation are among the three most widely practiced relaxation and self-regulation techniques in the West.

Hans Selye and Stress Research

In the mid 1900's, Hans Selye began his research on stress and the General Adaptation Syndrome (GAS), demonstrating how chronic strain on the body would create a generalized syndrome that passed through three distinct stages: 1. Alarm reaction, 2. Stage of resistance and, 3. Stage of Exhaustion (Selye, 1956). This research stimulated tremendous interest of what was termed "stress" and thousands of research studies have investigated ways of reducing stress and preventing the GAS, particularly intervening at stage two, the resistance stage.

A general point to be made here is that this research on stress further validates the important role of homeostatic mechanisms for healthy regulation of our psychophysiology and that when these mechanisms are brought out of balance, the GAS is automatically elicited.

Biofeedback and Systems Theory

Biofeedback, used to provide feedback of biological processes evolved, theoretically, from general systems theory. Systems theory is concerned with the behavior of any system and the idea that behavior emerges from dynamic interaction of the system's parts. Biofeedback is also based on a subfield of general systems theory, called cybernetics. Cybernetics is primarily concerned with how a system self-regulates. Further, biofeedback is concerned with dysregulation and the ensuing disorder and disease that follows (Schwartz, 1981). This theoretical context is, of course, no different than the theory behind mind-body self-regulation that has been presented thus far. What is somewhat unique in the case of biofeedback training is that the feedback mechanism is external to the person, not internal. In actuality, the use of external feedback mechanisms is really not that unique to biofeedback. For example, the therapist serves as an external feedback process for the client. Similarly, when we wish to learn something, we look for "experts" to give us feedback on our progress.

Cybernetic theory states that "a variable cannot be controlled unless information about the variable is available to the controller. When the variable to be controlled belongs to the controller and when information about the variable is presented to the controller, this completes a feedback loop" (Gardner, 1979, pp. 47-48). It is this feedback loop that is the essence of biofeedback (and psychophysiologic self-regulation).

Biofeedback is a training modality through which people can learn voluntary control over various physical systems and mental states. The application of biofeedback represents a merger of multiple disciplines, with interest derived from many sources: Behaviorism, cognitive neurosciences, applied psychophysiology, body therapies, meditation, self-actualization, etc. The goals of biofeedback are to develop an increased awareness of relevant internal physiological functions, to establish control over these functions, to generalize control from experimental or clinical settings to everyday life, and to achieve mind-body integration.

The biofeedback instrument is equipped with auditory and/or visual indicators that report the client's internal responses, such as muscle tension, heart rate, etc. As the client makes an attempt to change the current levels, the auditory or visual feedback informs him or her what actually occurs; in other words, whether he or she was able to change the levels in the desired direction, the opposite direction, or nothing changed. Through practice and the feedback, the client learns what they need to do to elicit the desired changes. For example, the client may be asked to tense and relax muscles while observing the EMG; then, they may be prompted to relax the muscles more and more each time they stop tensing. The EMG will indicate whether they are succeeding. The following diagram depicts the feedback process:

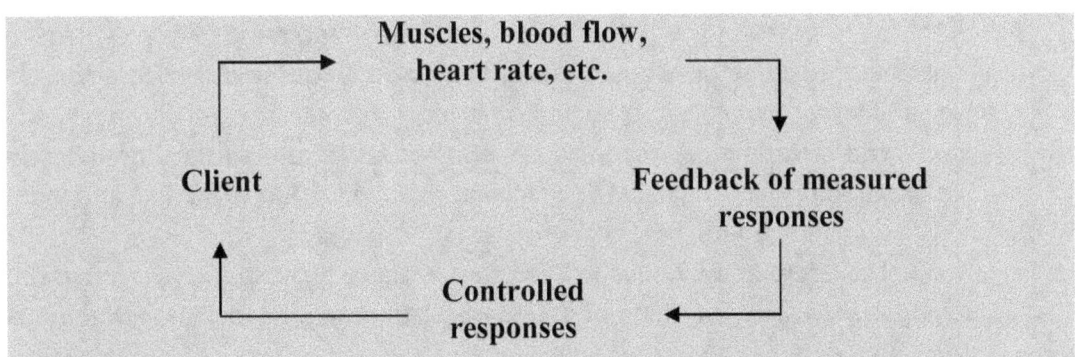

The excitement about biofeedback lies not just in understanding of feedback loops, but also in the application to biological functions thought previously to be beyond voluntary control and, further, that the utilization of electronic instruments can be used to accurately measure this control. This latter issue is particularly unique to biofeedback and has served to help validate a person's ability to consciously self-regulate mind-body processes.

While some therapists may be somewhat leery of using "machines" in therapy, it is prudent to understand the important role biofeedback can play in the therapy process. Biofeedback can serve as an objective validation of what the client is experiencing, rather than his or her problem being "all in the head." Of particular benefit is that through blinking lights, sounds, or digital readouts, clients are given specific and imme-diate feedback on their progress toward self-regulation.

Biofeedback, when used as a single clinical approach, is often not that effective. It can, however, be very effective when used in conjunction with specific relaxation and imagery techniques and exercises. In a further section of this manual, you will learn how to use biofeedback as part of an overall program of mind-body self-regulation.

Integrating the Various Investigations

Most of these investigations can be integrated within the context of self-regulation. Within this context, we consider four general parameters:

1. It is helpful to think of people as mind-body systems. The investigations of Western researchers and Asian practices support the view that our under-standing of how to help a person is greatly enhanced when we take the posi-tion that we need to address clients as mind-body systems.

2. People function as homeostatic systems. There exists innate mechanisms for keeping mind-body in a state of health. However, these homeostatic mecha-nisms can become dysregulated, creating stress and resulting in emotional and physical health problems. For example, this dysregulation can occur through upsetting the natural biological rhythms and in the development of the General Adaptation Syndrome.

3. Humans are capable of self-regulation of the body and mind. We can learn to consciously regulate previously involuntary and subconscious processes. Self-regulation has proven effective for a variety of organic, psychosomatic, and psychiatric disorders. A second role is in accessing and stimulating the self-actualization process. Here, we go beyond the elimination of disease and focus on the human need for personal growth.

4. Biofeedback, relaxation, concentration, and imagery techniques have proven to be especially useful for mind-body self-regulation and, hence, improving func-tional disorders.

2

Developing a Mindfulness Perspective of Self-Regulation

Purpose of this Chapter

Providing the therapist with clear rationales related to the benefits of these skills

Providing rationales that can be discussed with the client for increased understanding and motivation

Giving more clarity to the mind-body phenomenon in positive mental health

Understanding how the body can eventually serve as a highly sensitive biofeedback instrument

Understanding the various positive emotional states that can be acquired

Understanding how the mind can be better controlled

Introduction

Learning to be more mindful can mean a lot of different things. It is used in this chapter in two specific ways. First, it means that to really benefit from these stress reduction strategies and techniques, both the counselor and client need to understand all of the various benefits that are possible. Grasping this knowledge, along with contemplating how this knowledge can be used, will bring you into a more mindful state toward these approaches. Second, one of the benefits of the actual practices is to help you become more mindful and to maintain and deepen this state during daily living, as well as when facing stressful situations.

The use of relaxation, therapeutic imagery, and biofeedback are particularly effective when used together. These three modalities, when juxtaposed procedurally, support and strengthen each other. Biofeedback and relaxation, for example, inevitably make use of imagery to achieve results. For example, when wanting to relax one's muscles, it is helpful to feel the natural weight of one's body (use of imagery). This can also be made more direct by exaggerating the feeling of weight; for example, by feeling where the various areas of the body touch the surface they are sitting or lying on. However, a client may still find this difficult. They may find it more helpful to create a different image, such as imagining various parts of their body as "bags of sand," or imagining themselves as "sinking down into the surface they are lying on."

Through the use of imagery, clients can learn to relax very effectively and this will be further enhanced by direct feedback on their progress through biofeedback training. Imagery is also greatly enhanced by relaxation training. This is because relaxation helps to reduce conscious thought processes, allowing the mind to naturally shift to a less thinking and more spontaneous state. This is the more ideal state for beginning to work with habitual psychological patterns or in helping the client be aware of specific aspects of him or herself. This inward focus helps them get more easily in touch with the spontaneous imagery within themselves.

Turning to biofeedback, a client's success with this intervention is directly dependent on their success with relaxation. This is because relaxation is also a form of self-regulation and the kind of self-regulation that helps in controlling the body. Without relaxation training the client would struggle, not knowing except by pure trail-and-error how to proceed in the right direction clinically. This is why it is particularly useful to train the client in both modalities simultaneously.

When we compare biofeedback with relaxation or imagery, we find that biofeedback is an indirect process for gaining self-regulation in that it uses instruments external to the person for helping him or her self-regulate. However, the indirectness should not be viewed negatively. It has certain advantages, such as its ability to measure very subtle internal processes and its ability to always be totally objective. When a client practices a particular relaxation technique, they have only subjective experience, but very little objectivity in which to compare their experience against any standard norm.

For example, when practicing the Progressive Relaxation technique, a client may state that they can feel lower levels of tension, as well as being able to release muscular tension. But how do you or the client know exactly what kind of results are being obtained? The therapist who has years of experience with the particular technique can get pretty good at judging where the client is clinically, but can never be exactly sure. By attaching sensors to specific muscle groups, you and the client can know the exact level of tension, as well as the client's degree of muscular awareness. This results in a more accurate, systematic, and therefore more expedient approach toward the goal of relaxation and control of the neuromuscular system.

Through continued practice, the client begins to accurately judge their success, being able to correlate their subjective experience with the biofeedback measurements (along with the therapist feedback). While biofeedback has been extremely useful up to this point, the client soon reaches a time in therapy where the biofeedback instruments must be abandoned in favor of reliance on direct internal processes. At this stage, one is learning to rely on body as biofeedback, a topic discussed later. Relaxation and imagery, however, are never abandoned but, instead, are "honed" and developed toward fine-tuned skills, availing themselves as powerful agents for self-healing and growth.

Core Therapeutic skills Attained by Client

The primary theoretical assumption that forms the basis of this manual is the belief that most mental disorders are a result of a dysregulation. This belief is supported from a variety of sources, such as from traditional psychodynamic theory, which states that when a person is subjected to stress, the balance of forces making up the natural equilibrium is severely altered through changes in either the instinctual components or in the ego structures that control them, or both. While psychodynamic theory views this equilibrium issue as mostly psychological, other research, such as by Selye, included the biological realm as well. Increasingly, the view has evolved that any disequilibrium is, in actuality, a mind-body phenomena.

Working with this assumption, the issue becomes how to create equilibrium where disequilibrium has occurred. This author takes the stance that this is achieved via conscious self-regulation, a goal that most therapeutic approaches attempt in their own way to accomplish. This is seen as a two-step process. Regardless of the symptom, or the therapeutic approach, there are some core skills that will greatly serve the client along the road to conscious self-regulation. This is why self-regulation training should be initiated as early as possible in the therapy process. With this first step accomplished, the client is now ready for the second step of more in-depth clinical intervention. Let us now explore some of these core skills that will go a long way toward helping the client achieve self-regulation.

A. Calming the Mind-Body System

Charles Stroebel (1979), the developer of the Quieting Response, has his clients repeat the phrase, "Alert Mind-Calm Body." When this is used in combination with other exercises, clients are able to shift into a more adaptive psychophysiological state, called the "Quieting Reflex." This phrase, "alert mind-calm body" is not only a cognitive statement to be repeated to oneself, but most importantly, it is the goal; not only of Stroebel's technique, but for most, if not all, relaxation and related techniques for achieving low arousal and a re-balancing of homeostatic mechanisms. Alert mind and calm body can be thought of as a special state of memory, learning, emotions, thoughts, and behavior: The client is mentally clear, focused, with good concentration, along with a calm, relaxed body.

This is not a state that most people, without proper training, are able to attain naturally, except for brief periods of time. Yet for anyone who is able to shift into the alert mind and calm body state, they report that it is an extremely pleasant and rewarding experience.

There are, of course, varying degrees of skill in developing the alert mind and calm body state. Most clients find that it is not that difficult to develop, with practice, the ability to shift into this state when they are in non-threatening situations. But the goal is to develop the state to the degree that one is able to function this way throughout the day, even during times of stress. This is one's ability to generalize or transfer the skill and is where most clients have difficulty. However, with continued practice, this ability usually does improve. The alert mind and calm body state can and may need to be enhanced through the use of other therapy approaches used concurrently with re-laxation training, something you will need to judge as you work with particular clients.

Besides the ability to relax at will and to stay more calm and alert during times of potential stress, there are two other reasons for helping clients attain the alert mind and calm body state:

- Breaking the habitual stress patterns that are tied to subconscious issues. When the human system is calm, there is less triggering of subconscious issues and the stress patterns that manifest from these issues. The benefits of this should be obvious. A quick example is when working with a client who becomes extremely anxious in stressful situations. If this client is able, as a skill, to stay more calm, then his or her anxiety is less likely to be triggered. Theoretically, this is because a person cannot be anxious and relaxed at the same time and if the ability to relax is developed sufficiently, then the anxiety will not arise to the degree that it poses a problem. There is additional support for this view from psychodynamic theory, where it is believed that anxiety and/or depression arises first in response to stressors and that this, in turn, upsets the balance of psychic elements and structures. Therefore, keeping the system more calm prevents the triggering of the initial anxiety and depression that arises because of stress.

- Self-growth is naturally elicited. Maslow and others have theorized that when basic needs are met, one is naturally drawn to self-actualization. Calming the mind-body system serves to relax those basic needs that are triggered by stress and subconscious issues. This, in turn, frees one psychologically to pursue more growth-oriented goals. To some extent, the awareness of self-actualization issues arise automatically during relaxation training. Clients become more conscious of the self-growth goals and processes that exist within them when they are more calm. This awareness, then, usually induces a natural attraction toward these goals.

B. Homeostasis and the Autonomic Nervous System

"Homeostasis" has to do with the body's natural ability to maintain steady states. For example, heart rate, blood pressure, resting muscle tension, etc., have physiological governors to make sure that these systems or subsystems do not deviate beyond healthy limits. Chronic stress and other factors can cause these physiological systems to become chronically deregulated. Homeostatic re-regulation is needed when this happens.

From our earliest years of research on stress, we have known that the autonomic nervous system (ANS) plays a central role in stress. The ANS extends out from the brain through the spinal column and regulates the internal organs, such as breathing, heart functioning, digestion, musculoskeletal system, etc. In addition, it regulates the endocrine system and is responsible for sending pain and other signals to the brain for processing. When stress is experienced in the body, it is in the ANS where this stress is taking place.

The ANS consists of two subsystems, the sympathetic and parasympathetic.

The sympathetic arouses the body, causing particular glandular secretions, muscles to tense, heart to race, etc. The parasympathetic has the opposite effect, slowing the system down. These two subsystems function kind of like a teeter totter, one subsystem being more dominant one moment, then the other, then a balance between the two, and so forth.

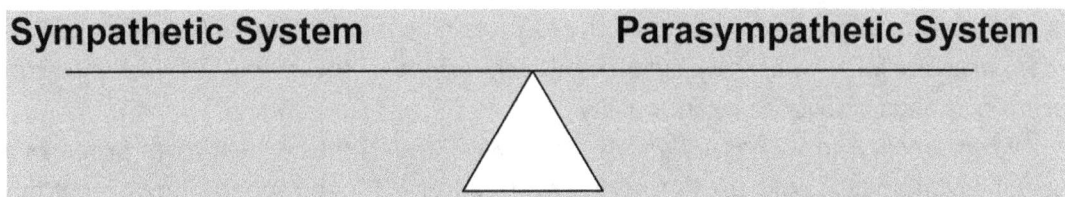

As the client learns to regulate stress levels, there is a natural balancing that occurs in the ANS (homeostatic re-regulation), allowing the two subsystems to shift naturally, then returning to a balanced state. In this way, the ANS is kept in a more flexible, spontaneous state, allowing physiological changes to occur in response to one's activity in the environment. Keep in mind that this balancing is not just physical, it is also psychological. Not only will blood pressure, heart rate, breathing patterns, muscular tension, etc., begin to normalize, but psychological processes tend to correct themselve too. With continued practice, there is a more permanent re-balancing of homeostatic systems and, therefore, mind-body processes.

Here is another example of how this can occur: I remember a number of years ago when I first began teaching relaxation and was conducting group relaxation sessions at a psychiatric hospital. After one of the sessions, a woman approached me with a smile on her face. She said that during the 30-40 minute relaxation session, her depression lifted for the first time in six months. While I knew that this was a temporary phenomenon, I also knew that there was something powerful about relaxation in its ability to produce such a dramatic, albeit temporary, effect. Since this first early experience, I have found this kind of dramatic re-balancing to be commonplace. I simply treat it as temporary, but also a sign of progress toward eventual more permanent re-balancing of the maladaptive systems.

Such examples only serve to prove the validity of how calming the mind-body system via the ANS can produce homeostatic balance. This, of course, does not preclude the need for additional therapy approaches. Calming the mind-body system is one important component, but other methods can and need to be used to enhance the effects. With some clients, calming the system is extremely difficult in the beginning and other methods should be initiated first. When addressing the issue of calming the mind-body system, I should mention that there are, in fact, at least two phases of this process. The first phase, which is the deep state of low arousal, must come first. When this is developed as a skill, then the second phase, what may be described as "relaxation-in-action" is taught. This is a generalization of the first level into day-to-day situations and, as stated, is the most difficult to develop. Other techniques, such as meditation, should come only after these first two phases are attained. These first phases serve as a necessary foundation for other advanced skills, a fact often not understood or ignored in many training programs.

C. Strengthening Intentionality

"Intentionality" generally refers to the mind's ability to be about, to represent, or stand for something. It also refers to the idea that the mind is always active; the mind's most primary form of activity is to cognitively orient in some way. We refer to this primary mental activity as intentionality.

Intentionality, and its associations with "will" and "volition," fell from grace as a useful psychological concept during the past century. More recently, however, it has re-emerged as a significant construct within the cognitive sciences. Intentionality has been particularly useful in explaining how themind selects and regulates cognitive processes.

Research in applied psychophysiology has also found that intentionality plays a central role in self-regulation. For example, Green, et al (1986) states: If the body affects the mind and the mind effects the body, how can anything happen except by reaction? Only by postulating the existence of volition [intentionality] can the logical bind be converted to a case of psychophysiologic constraints, rather than adamants.... When coupled with volition [intentionality], this principle allows a process called 'psychophysiologic-self regulation' to occur. (p.560)

Our mind generates mental activity from two forms of stimuli. One form comes from perceptual activity that is ordered and filtered according to physiological structures and mental belief systems, habits, etc. The second way is from memories, which is related to habitual perceptions, thinking, and feeling patterns. This is mentioned to clarify that when speaking about intentionality, I am relating it directly to these two sources of mental activity. Further, I am interested in the self-regulation of this mental activity. It appears that it is intentionality, among other mental processes, that enables a person to regulate the mental activity and the corresponding experiences that arise as a result. This idea is certainly not new, for it is discussed in Indian yoga and Buddhist texts dating back 2-4,000 years. We are only now beginning to understand the wisdom found in these and other such teachings and learn how to utilize these skills in clinical and educational settings.

Intentionality can be strengthened with training as part of an overall training program of self-regulation. Some authors, such as Assagioli (1961), have developed a variety of techniques for strengthening intentionality, particularly through the use of imagery. These techniques and exercises can be greatly enhanced through the training contained in this manual, particularly in the early stages of therapy. The training presented here should be considered a very effective way to start a client toward the discovery and strengthening of intentionality. The more abstract approaches to intentionality can be more easily understood and assimilated by clients once they have a concrete understanding.

D. Active-Receptive Attentional Skills

Like intentionality, there are certain psychological functions or processes that, while recognized as valid and important, are none-the-less difficult to investigate. Attention is one such process that psychologists have struggled to define or understand, yet recognize its central role in human consciousness. For example, Titchner afforded attention the central role in the entire psychological system.

Most investigators have some kind of definition of attention. Wundt called attention an inner activity that caused ideas to be present in consciousness to differing degrees. Pavlov referred to it as the orientation reflex. Berlyne stated that it refers to processes or conditions within the person that determine how effective a particular stimulus will be. America's first psychologist, William James, held three meanings for attention: As a selective process, an intensive process, and a sustaining process. Today, researchers tend to view attention in four ways: Attentional effort, spread of attention, selectivity, and shifting attention.

These four components of attention are particularly helpful when discussing ways to increase one's skill level with active-receptive attention. Interest in attention is most prominent in cognitive psychology. Two distinct approaches to the study of this process have developed: Information processing and self-regulation. Both approaches, however, go hand-in-hand when considered from a systems perspective where information processing is viewed as the communication that goes on within the human system and self-regulation is the control or regulation of the communication. Information processing attempts to trace the flow of information through the system and self-regulation attempts to control this flow of information. Additionally, information processing is interested in how attention plays a role in mental operations (memory, images, problem solving, etc.), while self-regulation is concerned with how to control the attentional process to enhance or change one's experience. Since this is a training manual, the interest is more in how the individual is able to control and change internal functioning. The self-regulation perspective, therefore, is more applicable within this context.

In the field of applied psychophysiology, the issue of attention has been an important one. One cannot really discuss self-regulation strategies without addressing this issue. Like Titchner, modern day researchers have found attention to be a central issue. Especially in the areas of relaxation and meditation, attention has proven central in understanding these two therapeutic strategies. For example, meditation differs from other relaxation practices along the dimension of attention and all of the different types of meditation involve the selective deployment of attention. In fact, Davidson and Goleman (1977) define meditation as the self-regulation of attention. At least a part of this belief is based on systems theory that says that a system controls its own states. This also helps in clarifying the relationship between intentionality, attention, and self-regulation.

Active Attention

More current research has found that attention can also be subdivided along the dimensions of active and receptive (Brown, 1977; Davidson and Goleman, 1977). Active attention requires various degrees of cognitive effort and discrimination. This is the kind of attention most people use in day-to-day tasks requiring any kind of mental effort and is the type of attention that is usually discussed by investigators of attention. It allows us to direct, select and then hold onto a single or related group of ideas, thoughts, images, or sensations. From a self-regulation point of view, it is crucial to consider active attention within the context of skill level rather than as a given. In other words, every person has a different ability to actively attend.

Returning to the four parameters of attention, each of these four should be considered when discussing a person's skill at active attention:

Regulation of Attentional Effort. First is the amount of effort or energy that is needed for the mind to control the attentional process. Different amounts of effort or energy are used in attentional control. However, this effort is not so much dependent on the difficulty of the task itself, from an objective standpoint, but is more dependent on individual factors. In other words, all people have varying degrees of active attentional ability; therefore, the amount of effort that is needed for a task will vary from individual to individual.

Regulation of the Spread of Attention: Narrow and Broad. Another parameter of attention is our ability to narrow our attention to very select stimuli, as well as the need to broaden our attention evenly over multiple stimuli. Specific examples of these two kinds of attention can be observed in our visual and auditory systems. Visually, we can focus on very specific visuals, referred to as focal vision, or broaden our focus toward what we call peripheral vision. Similarly, we can listen to very specific sounds, such as a person talking, or broaden our listening, such as when listening to an orchestra, where all of the instruments are heard as one piece of music. Interestingly, while all of us use both types of attention, there are also individual differences according to one's temperament. This is important to know because it can greatly influence how a client processes information. Some clients too often habitually focus on limited stimuli. This is common among those who struggle with anxiety, obsessive and compulsive tendencies, etc. There are also those who struggle with focusing on one thing at a time and tend to seek out high degrees of stimuli, something common in impulsive types, or those who struggle with controlling their emotions. This latter type can struggle with depression, mania, attention deficit/hyperactivity disorder, etc. The point to be made is that we all need to regulate the degree to which we spread our attention during different situations for optimal functioning. In spite of its relation to temperament, this attentional parameter can be trained in a more adaptive way.

Regulation of Attentional Selectivity. Selectivity refers to the ability to ignore irrelevant stimuli and to select only stimuli that is relevant to a given situation. This process appears to involve working memory, where a number of related processes are occurring simultaneously. Auditory distractions like noise and visual distractions such as movement can severely limit a person's ability to select relevant stimuli. As discussed with the previous attentional parameter, there are individual differences. For example, those with ADHD are found to be easily distracted by noise or too much visual stimulation. Research has shown, however, that people can be trained to improve attentional selectivity.

Regulation of the Ability to Shift Attention. Many clients struggle with the ability to shift their attention at will. In neuropsychology, this is related to the inability to shift attentional set; in other words, a person is attending to an event or situation and is unable to move the attention away from this to a new event or situation. This is common, for example, with brain trauma, ADHD, low cognitive functioning, OCD, etc, as well as in younger children. When working with clients who have this difficulty, it often appears to the professional that the person is just being stubborn when, in fact, he or she is struggling with a cognitive weakness related to attention. Again, however, clients can be trained to improve this ability.

These issues having to do with our ability to actively attend is tied to various factors just like other mind-body problems that may exist. For example, stress can greatly interfere with attention. This, in turn, can create more stress, forming a vicious cycle from which we can have trouble breaking out. The emphasis that I place on the factors presented here are somewhat unique in the field. They are, however, important for every therapist or counselor to understand and to consider as part of intervention.

Receptive Attention

Peper (1979) has clarified what he views as receptive attention:

> ...body control is achieved through passive attention and not trying, and...the important part of the control is the process and the attention to it-not the outcome or the goal. These dimensions operate in all physical, emotional, and mental activity.... But what is passive attention? It is doing without trying! It is allowing and directing without dictating.... Passive attention is the wedge through which we join our conscious and subconscious processes (pgs. 120-124).

Two simple examples of how passive attention is used by all of us on a day-to-day basis is going to sleep and urination. In both cases, we need to attend passively to the process. In doing so, we relax sufficiently to go to sleep or to start urinating. If one tries to force the process, they will only hinder it. "Trying" to go to sleep doesn't work; we need to allow ourselves to relax sufficiently to drift into a sleep state. Similarly, we have to relax the muscles of the bladder to allow urination to occur. Besides these above two examples, most people use receptive concentration only sporadically as they go through their day. Their general cognitive-behavioral habit patterns are one of high psychophysiological arousal, stimulated by caffeine, cigarettes, shallow breathing, high muscular tension, and environmental pressures. They are in a state of active attention, but this is weak and full of effort. They don't know that there is any such thing as attention without a stressful trying. Their eyes, face, and upper body display this stress brought on by strained effort. They are in a constant state of trying to "make" life be the way they want it to be, rather allowing themselves to "flow" with life in an attentive, non-stressed manner. It's like the person who says, "If I don't worry, who will?" He or she simply cannot imagine how to let go and experience life in an alert mind and calm body manner.

The benefit of receptive attention is in allowing us to access another parameter of the attentional process and, in so doing, enabling us to create greater health. Receptive attention needs to be utilized along with active attention in achieving a mind/body balance.

In conclusion to this discussion on active-receptive attention, I want to mention that some investigators (e.g., Luthe, 1976; Fehmi & Fritz, 1980) have the belief that active concentration is undesirable, that it produces stress and is maladaptive and that receptive attention should be the only desired attentional process. While I do not share this belief, it is somewhat understandable based on the potential problems of active attention discussed earlier. People's weak active attentional skills often do create stress, especially if they have also not developed their receptive attentional skills.

My own view is that both active and receptive attention are important and both need to be strengthened. This view has some support in the literature on meditation. Davidson & Goleman (1977), for example, says that one way to understand different types of meditation is to distinguish them in terms of whether their attentional strategy is more active or receptive. And Schuman (1980) also states: "These [research] results show that different meditation practices cultivate different attentional strategies" (p. 361).

If we turn to two rich sources of information on various practices utilizing attention and meditation, Indian yoga and Buddhism (especially Zen), we find a greater emphasis on active concentration techniques early on in their training and more receptive concentration techniques as the client progresses. For example, Kapleau (1965) says, "You are now ready to concentrate your mind. There are many good methods of concentration bequeathed to us by our predecessors in Zen. The easiest for beginners is counting incoming and outgoing breaths" (p.32). Although Zen meditation is, in general, considered to be more receptive in the attentional strategies used, even in advanced Zen practices, it is not devoid of active concentration. Kapleau relates the benefits of active concentration training for the general public:

> Through the practice of *bompu* [meaning "ordinary"] Zen you learn to concentrate and control your mind. It never occurs to most people to try to control their minds, and unfortunately this basic training is left out of contemporary education, not being part of what is called the acquisition of knowledge. Yet without it what we learn is difficult to retain because we learn it improperly, wasting much energy in the process. Indeed, we are virtually crippled unless we know how to restrain our thoughts and concentrate our minds. (1965, p. 42)

Shifting to Indian yoga, Eliade (1958) states that through the practice of breathing exercises (called *pranayamas*), we can greatly promote concentration skills. Eliade further states:

> The practice of *ekagrata* [concentration] tends to control...sense activity (*indriya*) and the activity of the subconscious (*samskara*). Control is the ability to intervene, at will and directly, in the functioning of these two sources of mental "whirlwinds" (*cittavrtti*). ...Through *ekagrata* one gains a genuine will--that is, the power freely to regulate an important sector of biomental activity. It goes

without saying that *ekagrata* can be obtained only through the practice of numerous exercises and techniques,...(1958, p.48)

The goal of active yoga and Zen attentional practices, though, is to enable the aspirant to develop the necessary skills to progress along the self-realization path. For yoga, it is sustained concentration that leads to meditation. For Zen, it is sustained concentration that leads to the "emptiness of mind" of zazen practice.

Whether one is in a state of active or receptive attention, I have found that relaxation and imagery are key factors in the development of effective and efficient concentration. For example, when actively concentrating on a task, it is important to calm the body systems as much as possible. A tense body will greatly hinder effective attention.

Interestingly, with regular practice, one finds that in a deep state of sustained concentration, it is quite easy to "shift into" a receptive attentional state. This might mean that active and receptive attention are somehow connected along some kind of continuum. Continued research may help in clarifying this issue. With skillful practice of active-receptive attention, a person goes through a natural qualitative mental shift, where there is more of a balance between the active and receptive consciousness and one is better able to shift, at will, to the particular attentional strategy that is needed for the task at hand. When we understand that different concentration practices cultivate different skills, we move closer to making use of the self-regulation of attentional strategies in clinical practice.

E. Becoming More Objective Toward Oneself

Another highly significant skill that this training can help a client develop is increased objectivity. When one is able to calm the inner system sufficiently to bring about low-arousal, there is a corresponding state-dependent experience that takes place. This was earlier referred to as the alert mind and calm body state but, in this case, refers primarily to the first level of relaxation, the deep state. This experience, which involves related memory, learning and behavior, allows the client, for this specific period of time, to experience an "ideal" state within him or herself that is seldom experienced. This ideal state allows the client to shift temporarily out of his or her traditional stress patterns and to experience a state of balance. For many clients, this level of training usually takes some real dedicated practice for at least a couple of weeks to be able to go in and out of a deep state with each practice.

Through the continued practice of coming in and out of this deep state, the client begins to sense the difference between this more ideal state and his or her more common stressed state. When coming out of a deep state of relaxation, clients frequently report experiencing old physical bracing patterns returning, as well as the return of habitual thoughts and feelings.

Inform your clients that where they need to focus most is:

The transition from the deep relaxation state to when the old habit patterns begin to return. I recommend that they focus on trying to carry this relaxed, more ideal state, with them into their daily living. With practice, they will find that they are able to do this with increasing frequency and depth of experience.

Finding a useful "anchor" that helps to connect them with this relaxation state. For example, when a client wants to shift to their alert mind and calm body state, they can put their forefinger and thumb of their dominant hand together. This "grounds" or anchors them psychophysiologically to the state dependent memory, learning and behavior of the relaxed state. Another anchor could be taking a deep breath, etc.

Tell them that *now that they are at this stage in their skill where they are much more aware of when they are relaxed and when they are experiencing their stress patterns*, that they will find themselves faced with a natural dilemma during day-to-day situations. This dilemma is in having to decide whether to choose relaxation or to allow themselves to fall into the same old patterns. For example, let's say that a client is having an argument with his girlfriend. He will likely, as a result of the training, become aware of how his anger tenses his body and that this feels quite uncomfortable. He may also notice how his anger has a subjective "cutting," or "burning" quality and that this is emotionally hurtful to his girlfriend. At this point, he has to make a decision as to whether to continue arguing and let the anger have its effect on the body and the other person, or to let go of having to "win" the argument in favor of maintaining a state of healthy relaxation.

Additionally, if this client has learned to reframe his view of himself in this type of situation, a positive kind of cognitive dissonance will be created between his habitual reaction of anger and his new reframed ideas about himself of, say, being calm and sensitive toward others. Further, if he has rehearsed cognitive-behavioral strategies ahead of time, he is more likely to begin to change this old habit pattern. Clinically, it is obvious that by integrating various strategies together you can greatly improve your client's ability to make positive changes. Increasing a client's objectivity also serves to increase his or her awareness of him or herself as well. Increased self-awareness is essential in producing true change. Any way that you can help this process will benefit the client. I have found that this training is a very good way to start expanding a client's awareness of him or herself, especially of the body consciousness. Other methods can be taught concurrently and subsequent to establishing this important foundation of relaxation.

F. Learning to Enjoy the Body and the Present Moment

Most of the time clients' minds are actively focused on thought processes related to work, school, family, social activities, watching television, listening to music, etc. In other words, their minds are occupied with thoughts that are related to events outside of themselves, not what is occurring in their inner environment at that moment. Even when they need to focus on the body, such as when showering, eating, exercising, etc., their minds usually focus on other things rather then the experience at hand. This lack of focus on the body, especially when the body's actions make up much of the activity, creates a psychological "flaw" in how a person is attending. This flaw tends to be habitual and encourages a variety of problems. In fact, there are at least three general problems that arise from this disconnection from the body's experiences:

- Mind-body dysregulation can occur. A person doing one thing while thinking of something else is creating a dichotomy and inconsistency in the mind-body system. The body reacts according to information provided from the mind. If this information is inconsistent with what the body needs to be doing, stress often occurs. A person sitting back in a chair while worrying about his or her future is, to use a metaphor, like driving a car with one foot on the brake and the other on the gas pedal. The body is held immobile even though the mental images suggest a threatening need to physically react (in this case, to prevent a problem with one's future). The result is physical and emotional tension. While we need to plan sometimes, this should occupy only a small part of our time. The rest of the time we need to be attuned what is currently happening at that moment. This helps us be aware of our immediate needs as they arise and enables us to send information to the body that is consistent with what the body is doing.

- A lack of sufficient body awareness can occur; therefore, any attempt at self-regulation becomes very difficult. When we focus our attention (using receptive attention) on the muscles or other parts of the body, we are literally strengthening the neuropathways between the brain and that part of the body. If our mind is thinking of something else, this does not occur. This is why we need to constantly remind the client to fully attend to whatever they are doing so that their awareness of the mind-body process can be strengthened and, consequently, their ability to self-regulate will also be strengthened.

- An inability to use the body as biofeedback. A person entirely focused within one's thoughts with little awareness of their body will not have the advantage of having the experiences in the body alert them as to subconscious processes. For example, your body may be showing stress in certain ways in response to external stressors, but you may not consciously be aware of the stress because you are blocking it from your consciousness. Therefore, you cannot benefit from the feedback that your body is trying to send you.

An example, using exercise, might help clarify these three problems. We often see people reading a book while walking on a treadmill or pedaling a stationary bike, listening to music while jogging, or without these obvious distractions, simply allowing his or her mind to wander from thought to thought. What we find here is that the person has found another way to ignore his or her body even while directly exercising it. What is occurring then is that the person is taken out of their present, moment-to-moment experience, and is separating the mental experience from the physical experience. This creates, what Barrell, et al (1985) calls "psychological sleep." We are failing to notice the world as it is directly presented to us and, therefore, are not in touch with what is actually happening. When we allow ourselves to just experience the body in its state of movement or breathing and when we allow ourselves to fully experience our present environment, we begin to "wake up" from this psychological sleep, attaining what it often referred to as "mindfulness." There is a Zen saying that relates to this process: "When you eat, just eat; when you walk, just walk." Through this fuller, more encompassing experience, we begin to develop a better understanding and joy of our own beingness. This is essential in helping us increase the quality of our existence.

G. Body As Biofeedback: The Mind's Own Mirror

In chapter one I discussed how mind-body is one system and that experience of body is really a psychological experience and, further, that to include body in counseling is, in actuality, to include another aspect of mind. I want to follow this view with another useful perspective: how the body serves a unique role of mind and, as such, can help mind become more aware of itself because of the body's ability to serve as feedback of information. And I want to discuss the benefits to both the client and therapist.

The uniqueness of the body is that it is very concrete, very "here." It can be seen, felt, heard. Of particular interest is that body, as a kind of simple mirror of the mind, lets us know what is going on, not only consciously, but also subconsciously. The body presents us with what we call "nonverbal cues": voice tone and quality, movement of eyes, facial expressions, changes in body posture or movements, changes in breathing, heart rate, blood pressure, blood flow, muscular bracing patterns, sweat gland activity, and on and on. Some of these cues can be externally observed by the therapist. Other cues can be observed (at least potentially) internally by the client. The therapist can also observe these cues within him or herself. While these cues are often called nonverbal, they could be more accurately defined as psychophysiological cues.

From this perspective, we know that there is a physiological response to every conscious thought or emotion. A single image floating through the mind creates a corresponding sensory-motor activity. Conscious thoughts and feelings, as well as subconscious feelings, strong habit patterns, etc., will immediately show themselves in the body. We often see this as habitual bracing patterns (raised shoulders, teeth grinding, etc), habitual thought processes, psychosomatic complaints, posture, habitual facial expressions, habitual voice patterns, etc. By understanding these responses, we see that the body can serve as a simple biofeedback instrument. It very accurately and nonjudgementally feeds back to the mind what is occurring physiologically and, indirectly, what is occurring in the conscious and subconscious mind. This is where this training is especially helpful.

Training in the strategies presented in this manual will help clients become more sensitive to their bodies so that they can begin to sense what their body is telling them. Clients become increasingly able to experience the subtle bodily processes that correspond to conscious and subconscious thoughts, feelings, and images. The therapist, of course, needs to guide them how to do this and to help them explore these mind-body experiences. With practice, clients can begin to understand what the feelings of anger, sadness, fear, anxiety, frustration, etc., feel like at more subtle levels and how they respond physiologically. This, in turns, helps them to recognize resistance, anxiety, and other psychological responses that arise in therapy.

For example, if while discussing a particular issue, clients become aware of their heart rate increasing, they will begin to recognize that they are emotionally reacting to something. Clients are taught that they cannot ignore these experiences, because to do so is to deny what their body is telling them. Common patterns, such as defense mechanisms (denial, rationalization, etc.), start becoming obvious to them, even though they might not know exactly what it is that's not right. But they are more likely to be open to the therapist's analysis or suggestions at these times. Overall, they will tend to be much more open to the therapy process.

It is very important that the therapist also practice and become adept at this same training. There are several reasons for this. One is that when a therapist uses certain methods, exercises, or techniques, he/she does not have a true sense of how these approaches are experienced by the client unless he/she has also practiced them. Consequently, it becomes difficult for the therapist to really guide the client through each step of the process because, as therapists, we need to have a real feel for what is happening inside the client.

A second point is that there is a lot of research these days demonstrating the significance of role playing and modeling. Therefore, a therapist who has achieved some mastery over these self-regulation processes is like a mirror, modeling for what the client needs to achieve. Clients are also more motivated when they can observe these qualities in the therapist. In addition, a rather obvious benefit is that if this training helps clients achieve the core therapeutic skills being presented in this section, it can also help the therapist develop these same skills.

Another benefit to therapists who practice this training (or some kind of related training) is that they become more skilled in observing various mind-body cues that are indicative of the mind-body patterns, behaviors, and the current processing that is going on in the client. This understanding is beneficial in general when helping a client therapeutically. Psychoanalysts understood this in describing the problems with transference and countertransference occurring during therapeutic process; this is why there was a belief that would-be analysts would benefit from going through analysis. To quote Bandler and Grinder (1975): "Respectful awareness of the capacity of the client's subconscious mind to perceive meaningfulness of the therapist's own subconscious behavior is a governing principle in psychotherapy" (p. 45). This ability of the client and therapist to be more aware of subconscious processes leads naturally to the next core therapeutic skill, increasing the ability to access the subconscious.

I have found this training to be particularly useful in the context of hypnotherapy, imagery, and other approaches where you are attempting to access the client's subconscious. This training will be beneficial in developing the skill of observing the mind-body cues that are used to guide the client along the therapeutic path and providing the kind of subconscious feedback from one's own psychophysiology that better serves the therapy process.

H. Accessing the Subconscious

By learning to recognize psychophysiological (or what we normally include as nonverbal) cues, the client is, in actuality, learning to access his or her subconscious. By including these cues within one's conscious   experience, one has expanded the mind into a previously subconscious realm, using the body as a feedback mechanism for this process. In this sense, the body is a kind of "door" or "link" to the subconscious.

By maintaining the alert mind and calm body state during the day and in therapy, the client will naturally be more in contact with what is happening at the subconscious level. This, of course, does not mean that one does not need to go "deeper" into the subconscious for therapeutic purposes, but simply that the client has found a way to begin to access the subconscious. This creates a foundation upon which other therapeutic methods can be more easily built. Clients who have mastered the skills of this training move much more quickly in accessing the deeper levels of the subconscious and are able to work through these related issues with less resistance and difficulty.

There is, yet, another benefit of this training when working through deeper issues. Sometimes, the process will get too intense for the client, both in the session and afterwards. The client needs to have the ability to control how intense one's experience is so they are not overwhelmed by it. Training which allows the client to achieve a degree of self-regulation can help to control the intensity of an experience. If an experience becomes too intense, the client can be taught to simply shift from it to a state of low-arousal or alert mind and calm body. In addition, teaching a client to utilize therapeutic imagery, along with calming one's system, can be especially effective. For example, once when I was taking a client through a hypnotherapy session using imagery, the client found herself in a room with no doors and began to panic. I gave the suggestion to simply relax and be more intentional in what she wanted to happen. I then suggested that she use her will to "mock-up," or imagine a door that she could exit from the room. She did this with no difficulty. Additionally, she reported in the following session that she felt she achieved an increased sense of inner strength and confidence by her ability to get control over this imagery experience. What could have been a frightening experience became, instead, one that helped her grow. Accessing at least the beginning levels of the subconscious can and should become a natural skill and can be achieved by most clients through this training.

Summary

We know that traditional therapies focus on the personality factors that impede growth and cause behavioral issues. While these therapies are helpful, they oftentimes *fail to tap into the client's motivational potential and sufficiently raise their level of awareness.* Consequently, we need to search elsewhere.

Mindfulness-based approaches can involve any number of strategies and methods, some that has been touched upon already, that can encourage motivation and increase awareness.

Regardless of the different approaches, there is a common mindset that includes:
- Non-judgmental
- Meta-cognitive awareness
- Receptive attention
- Detached awareness of internal events
- Keeping one's awareness alive to the present moment
- Open, flexible, creative mindset
- Balancing rational thought with perceptual awareness

3

Beginning Stages of Mindfulness Training

Purpose of this Chapter

Teach clients some simple, but helpful stress reduction and self-regulation strategies to be used throughout the day

Understand the significant role of our muscles and respiration in responding to stress

Understand how we can regulate these systems for the purpose of reducing chronic stress

Teach your clients simple stretching exercises for reducing chronic stress

Teach your clients a number of different kinds of breathing exercises for both reducing chronic stress and energizing the body

Teaching Simple Coping Strategies

In the beginning of treatment, it is helpful to teach some simple strategies for coping with stress that can be used throughout the day. Most of these suggestions can be practiced in just a couple of minutes and in most situations. They are especially helpful for those who are first learning relaxation.

7 Point Stress Check

As was discussed earlier, our own body can serve as a biofeedback device by letting us know exactly what is happening in our bodies and, therefore, indirectly what is happening with our emotions and thoughts. Here is a quick stress check for clients to use throughout the day to check on themselves. Clients will eventually learn which of these body areas indicate their particular stress so that they can focus on or attend to these key body points during the day and utilize relaxation strategies to correct the pattern.

Muscle Check:	Shoulders and neck tense?
	Jaw tight or sore?
	Tension between shoulder blades?
Temperature Check:	Hands or feet cold?
Perspiration Check:	Palms sweaty?
	Mouth dry?
Heart Check:	Heart pounding or irregular?
	Pulse rapid?
Breath Check:	Shallow?
	Rapid?
	Irregular?
Digestive Check:	System tense or upset?
Emotional Check:	Dwelling on worries?
	Flying off the handle?
	Getting upset easily?
	Is this the way I want to feel?

Note: Therapist: You might consider creating a small laminated card for the wallet or desktop.

Deep Breathing

Become aware of the breath and how it moves into the abdomen and chest
Focus on the inhalation & exhalation
Intentionally slow the breathing down
Emphasize doubling the exhalation over the inhalation
Slow breathing down as much as possible

Body Anchor Technique

When relaxing, we need to anchor the mind to the body.

Help client select a body anchor in advance. The body anchor should always be the same and practiced the same way each time.

Examples: placing the forefinger and thumb of dominant hand together; focus on the breath in a particular way; focus on the heart rate; feel the heaviness in the body.

For practice, start by becoming aware of your body.

Next, do your anchoring with full concentration.

Once you feel fairly anchored to your body, you can shift to a relaxation technique, self-talk strategy, etc.

The Beating Heart Concentration & Relaxation

This can serve as an anchoring technique or extended as relaxation practice.

Place your dominant hand on your chest and try and feel the beating sensation.

Practice following the beating at least 1 minute and preferably around 3 minutes.

When extended into a relaxation technique, the objective is to slow the heart rate down.

Tense-Slow-Relax Technique

This is a variation of Jacobsen's Progressive Relaxation (taught in more detail later).

Review ahead of time the major muscle groups: Arms and hands, shoulders, neck, upper, mid, and lower back, stomach, buttocks, legs and feet.

Practice scanning the body for muscle tension, or go through all major muscles.

Focus on the particular muscle with full concentration.

Feel the muscle tensing up and hold for several seconds.

Slowly release the muscle tension while continuing to focus on the specific area.

Feel the muscle becoming relaxed, with a feeling of lightness in that area.

If tension still exists, repeat. Repeat as many as 3-4 times as necessary.

Go to the next muscle group and repeat above procedures.

Calm Scene Technique

Visual imagery can be effective in shifting negative thoughts and feelings toward more positive experiences.

Talk to the client about positive images that are very relaxing and develop one or two images ahead of time.

Examples: the beach, in the woods, relaxing by a stream, playing music, doing art, etc.

Have the client image the scene and allow the scene to change as it wants, enjoying the feeling of relaxation and calmness that the scene induces.

Remain with the scene as long as is necessary to produce desired effects.

Walking to Calm Down Technique

This might seem like an obvious strategy, but many people don't think to walk when upset.

Sometimes the best approach may be to calm down by removing oneself from the situation (to avoid losing control).

This is discussed with the client (as to time, place, etc.).

Specify a period of time, usually at least 10 minutes.

Walk to process and clear your head of worrisome or other negative thoughts and to problem solve.

Utilize the walking breathing technique for further benefit (see later).

Five Minute Relaxation

Lay or sit down in a comfortable chair. Arms at your side, palms facing upward. Preferably keep the eye closed. Legs uncrossed, toes pointing slightly outward. Legs and arms are not touching your body. Relax jaw. Feel your breathing, watching your breath for a couple of minutes. Next, feel the entire body becoming very heavy against the surface that you are lying on, allowing the heaviness to grow in intensity. Continue this for a couple of minutes. Finally, feel both breathing and heaviness. When you are ready to get up, stretch your muscles, take two deep breaths, and open your eyes.

Stop and Breathe

Whenever you notice disturbing or anxiety-provoking thoughts, internally shout "Stop!" to yourself. Imagine hearing your voice with a lot of authority to it.

Shift your attention to your breathing. Begin taking slow, deep breaths into your diaphragm. Place a hand on your abdomen to make sure it is expanding with each breath.

Now start counting your breaths. As you exhale, count one. As you exhale again, count two. Keep counting up to four. Each time you reach four, start over again at one. Try to keep your mind as empty as possible as you focus on counting each breath. Continue until you feel relaxed and repeat each time you feel stress coming on.

Basic Cognitive Restructuring Procedures

Changing Channels

Use the same thought-stopping procedure as in the previous exercise.

As soon as you have interrupted the stressful cognition, use a pre-rehearsed visualization to block the return of any unwanted thoughts. Make sure the visualization is something you can elicit easily without struggle. For example: Imagine a radio and that different thoughts are at different frequencies. Imagine turning the knob to change the channel from negative thoughts to more positive ones.

Once you feel more calm, shift to more positive or problem solving thinking and, if your mind begins to entertain negative thinking again, repeat exercise.

Talk it Out Technique

Many people calm down by talking out their problem.

This can prevent the client from losing self-control.

Talking it out can be structured with therapist and pre-taught.

Specify a period of time, usually not exceeding 10 minutes. Longer talking can be done at other more appropriate times.

Self-Talk Technique

This uses the power of thought to regulate emotions and physical responses.

Based on the client's presenting issues, select with client self-statements that will most likely help them to calm down and let go of stressful thoughts, feelings, or bodily tension.

Examples: "I am relaxed," "My body is calm," "Nothing bothers me," I'm staying cool," etc.

Have client practice frequently throughout day.

Irrational Thinking

Almost all negative, irrational and unhelpful self-talk can be categorized into one of the following types of statements:

"Should" Statements

"I should have more money"

"Awfulizing" Statements

"Its awful the way other people act toward me"

"Catastrophizing" Statements

"This is horrible, this is going to ruin my life"

Need Statements

"I need to have x, y, z (which are really wants and not needs)"

Human Worth Statements

"I am a complete screw-up for making a mistake"

Help clients explore the irrationality of these statements and in what ways they tend to use them. Then explore ways to replace the negative statements with more positive ones.

Stretching for Relaxation and Energizing the Mind-Body System

Introduction

The design of our neuromuscular system is to help support our body, provide proper movement, and physically engage the environment. These active physical processes are also intertwined with our psychological states, as Rolf (1977) points out:

> Through movement, humans sense the driving force of change. Movement is the physical acceptance of change; awareness of this tends to be below the individual's conscious awareness. For the therapist of the psyche as well as for the therapist dealing with the physical man, the goal is appropriate movement. The psychotherapist senses immobility in the dimension of time rather than of space. The individual bogged down, unmoving in time, unable to escape from his infantile or adolescent assumptions or traumata, manifests this physically as well as psychologically. His lack of movement, his general or localized rigidity, are unequivocal in their statement. Movement induced in the physical body... will loosen psychological chains. The job of the psychotherapist thus becomes easier. (Rolf, p. 153)

By understanding the role of the different physical systems of the body, we can better understand this intimate relationship to our psychological states and how, by working with the body, we can impact the mind.

Striated muscles cover most of the outside of the body and make up approximately 40% of the average person's weight. And every major muscle group in our body is sensitive to and reacts to stress. Therefore, it is an extremely important system to self-regulate for optimal mind-body functioning. There are many excellent methods for working with the neuromuscular system, so what I want to do is explain the purpose behind these various methods for your own information and in answering your client's questions or in directing their progress.

In general, the striated muscles need to be strong and relaxed. When a muscle is strong (through regular toning and strengthening exercises) it is able to support the body and protect it from many of the stresses that can impinge upon it. And, when a muscle is relaxed, it is at its maximum length, giving it flexibility and pliability. Relaxed muscles also encourages a calm mental state. Relaxed muscles will also be rested and, therefore, able to react quickly and effectively. Strong, relaxed muscles act like "shock absorbers" for the body, supporting and buffering it from stressors.

When particular muscles are not strong or relaxed, they have difficulty supporting the body and poor, weak posture can result, as well as the development of certain neuromuscular disorders. Weak, tense muscles can come about from different sources: a lack of proper exercise, poor posture, poor body mechanics, poor diet, or from emotional issues where the stress to the muscles comes from chronic bracing, tensing, etc.

Since weak, tense muscles can come about as a result of either internal or external factors, both factors need to be addressed. This should also be accomplished in a systematic way so as to achieve maximum results. This is why, for example, it is recommended that deep muscle stretching be practiced first, followed by Progressive Relaxation.

Points to Remember and Emphasize with clients:

Muscles need to be strong and relaxed.

Toning/strengthening exercises need to done regularly and your client may need additional individual exercises that pertain to posture.

Emotional stress can create muscular tension and weakness.

Poor posture can create muscular tension and weakness.

Stretching exercises need to be done at least daily and, preferably, two times per day. Targeted muscle groups may need more frequent stretching.

A few simple, but effective stretches are provided which target common uscle groups that are particularly sensitive to and often become tense due to stress. It is recommended that these four points are followed by the client if they are to achieve effective results:

Concentrate on the muscles you are stretching, avoiding other thoughts. Focus on feeling exactly which muscles are being stretched, keeping your concentration only on these muscles. This ability will deepen with practice.

Do all of the stretches very slowly and smoothly. The slower, the better. No rough or jerky movements.

Never hold the breath, except temporarily as indicated. Steady breathing encourages concentration, enhances the ability to sense the muscle, and greatly helps in the release of tension. A person will spontaneously exhale with the release of tension if the breath is kept free and relaxed.

If the prescribed length of time for a stretch creates too much discomfort, reduce the time. Increase the time only as you improve.

These points should be addressed continually in the beginning of training to assure compliance. I also have included a "benefits" section with each exercise to help guide you in prescribing exercises and determining if the results are being achieved.

Neck Stretch

First put your attention on the neck muscles. Then slowly drop your head to the right side as you exhale, letting your head hang toward your shoulder by only the force of gravity. Inhale and exhale naturally, but every time you exhale, imagine the left side of the neck muscles stretching further, allowing the head to drop closer to your shoulder. Don't force this; just use your imagination and the muscles will let go on their own as they are ready. Continue this for 12 to 15 seconds. Do the same movement to the left side, feeling the right side of the neck stretching. Now bring your head back to its original starting position and feel the muscles continuing to relax for several seconds. Repeat exercise 1 to 2 times.

Now slowly turn you head to the right, as if you are trying to look behind you. Stretch around and stop when it gets uncomfortable. Hold for 8 to 10 seconds, breathing in and out naturally. Again imagine the neck muscles stretching further every time you exhale. Do the same movement to the left. Now bring your head back to the front position and feel the muscles continuing to relax for several more seconds. Repeat 1-2 times.

Benefits: All types of headaches; upper body stress; poor upper body posture; chronic anxiety; TMJ syndrome; some claim that it can also help stimulate and energize the thyroid gland.

Modified Neck Roll

Making mental contact with the neck muscles, allow your head to drop all the way forward allowing the muscles to go as loose and limp as possible. Breathing slowly, begin to very slowly turn your head to the right, as if you were rolling it around, feeling the fluidity of the movement. Continue to come around about 45 degrees past the right shoulder. Stop there and start the movement back toward the front, continuing toward the left to the same 45 degree position past the left shoulder. Stop there and start the movement back again. When you reach the original forward starting position, raise your head and continue to feel the neck muscles relaxing for several seconds. Repeat 1 to 2 times. Each repetition should take 60-80 seconds, which gives you an idea of how slow your head movement should be. Most people tend to do this exercise much too quickly, so practice slowing it down. To clarify how far you should turn the head in each direction, think of the head as being able to turned 360 degrees. You are turning it 270 degrees, eliminating the 90 degrees where the head would drop all the way back; a position that could strain the neck a little too much, especially if you've had a neck injury.

Benefits: Same as for "Neck Stretch."

Shoulder Pump

Make mental contact with your shoulder muscles. Then as you inhale, slowly draw your shoulders upward toward your ears, keeping your arms relaxed and limp. Hold the position for about 5 seconds while feeling the tension in the shoulder muscles. Now begin to exhale while pumping the shoulders up and down. Continue to feel the shoulders relaxing more and more for several seconds as they remain limp. Repeat 1 to 2 times.

> **Benefits**: Chronic pain in neck, shoulders, and upper back; headaches; poor upper body posture; chronic anxiety. Also increases awareness of chronic raising and holding the shoulders, especially during times of stress.

Overhead Stretch

Stand with your feet about shoulder length apart and bring your attention to your chest, upper back, shoulders, arms, as well as your ankles and calves. Now bring your arms straight over your head as if you were reaching upward. As you inhale, go up on your toes and stretch your arms upward as far as possible, feeling the above mentioned muscles being stretched. Hold about 5 seconds. Now exhale, drop your arms, and bring your heals to the floor all in one motion, feeling your whole upper body go limp. Rest, feeling the stretched muscles relaxing more and more over the next several seconds. Repeat 1-2 times.

> **Benefits:** Same as the "Shoulder Pump," plus tension in the upper arms, chest, mid-back, calf and ankle areas.

Spinal Twist

Stand with your feet 2 to 3 feet apart. Make mental contact with your spine and, breathing freely, begin to swing your arms from side to side, allowing the arms to swing loosely and freely. Feel your spine twisting, as if you were attempting to look behind you as you turn from side to side. Make sure your arms are relaxed, allowing them to wrap around your body as you twist. Feel the muscles stretching the entire length of the spine. Continue for 8 to 12 seconds. Rest if you begin to feel dizzy, then try again, or find a centering point behind you to focus on as you twist around.

> **Benefits:** Any chronic back pain or tension is helped by this exercise. This is a very good exercise for keeping the spine loose and flexible. You will hear a lot of "cracking" of the spine as the vertebrae are re-adjusted.

Shoulder Rotation

Standing, extend your arms outward at your sides at shoulder level, palms facing upward. Bring your awareness to your shoulders. Now, bending your arms at the elbows, touch your fingertips to the top of your shoulders. Begin to move the elbows in a circular pattern, rotating the shoulder joints. Do this 10 times in each direction. Make the circular motion as large as possible, bringing the elbows together in front of the chest.

> **Benefits:** The same as the "shoulder pump." This exercise also rotates the shoulder joints much better than any other exercise, so it is helpful for those with severe joint problems, such as arthritis.

Forward Bend

Standing with your feet 6-12 inches apart, make mental contact with your lower back, the back of your legs, and your upper back. With your knees slightly bent, bend forward as you exhale, allowing the top half of your body to hang loosely, especially your arms. Be aware of how relaxing this position is for the upper part of your body, and how it stretches the lower back and back of the legs. Every time you exhale, imagine the body dropping forward more and more. Hold position 12 to 15 seconds. Now inhale as you slowly raise your body back up, keeping your arms relaxed. Keep mental contact with the body and feel the tension continually releasing over the next several seconds. Repeat 1-2 times.

> **Benefits:** This is helpful for chronic low back pain, for stretching the mid and upper back, back of the legs, and for relaxing the muscles in the shoulders, and arms.

Regulating the Respiratory System

The ability to become very aware of and learn to control an aspect of the autonomic nervous system is generally only possible by indirect means. This is why the respiratory system is so important in achieving self-regulation. It is the only major autonomic system over which a person can have direct awareness and control.

Our respiration works automatically. But, at any moment, we can change our breathing patterns through the use of our voluntary control, just like our control over the musculoskeletal system. The yogis, monks, and folk medicine healers of the East have known this for thousands of years and, in the last 50 years, much of this knowledge has been made available to Western health care practitioners.

In the West, we are beginning to understand the role of respiration as never before. For example, physiologist Rolf (1977), founder of the Rolfing technique, states: "Contrary to the general idea, normal respiration in a balanced body involves movement not merely in the thorax, but from the sacrum all the way to the cranium. In normal inspiration, the spine lengthens from one end to the other; in expiration, it shortens" (p. 153). Brena, a physician, (1972) also states:

> Following a regular, slow, and deep breathing, the oxygenation of the blood is known to improve consistently; in consequence, the internal respiration also improves. In other words, regular, harmonious breathing rhythms do improve our tissue carburation. However, few of us are capable of breathing in a really harmonious way. Our voluntary control over the respiratory movements is quite limited, being mostly governed by unhealthy habits of living (p. 90).

The importance of healthy breathing is becoming increasingly more obvious. Essentially, the benefits can be divided into three categories:

General health of the organism through proper oxygenation of all the cells of the body. This includes efficient combustion as well as the elimination of carbon dioxide and other waste substances. Proper nutrition is also important in providing high quality "fuel" for the body.

Energy efficiency. Our breathing patterns are directly connected to our energy levels. Since we are an energy system, it should be quite obvious why this is so tremendously important. And as anyone who performs somekind of aerobic exercise on a regular basis knows, we can increase our energy levels. And cigarette smokers also know what deficient breathing can do to their energy levels.

Reduced stress. A calm mind and relaxed body is always accompanied by a rather slow and regular respiration, whereas stress causes a speeding up of the heart and breathing patterns, which further increases anxiety. Brena (1972) makes this point very clear:

> This is a matter that characterizes successful men [and women] in every field of human activity: no great general on the battlefield, no important industrialist

at work, no famous orchestra conductor on the platform, has heart palpitations and difficulty breathing before making a decision with an objective mind (p.84).

The *Hatha* yogins go even a step further in stating the benefits of proper breathing. They feel that breathing is directly related to the essential "life force" of the body, called *prana*. It is claimed that through breathing exercises, called *pranayamas*, this life force can be controlled and used to enhance a person's health and well-being. While the existence of *prana* has yet to be proven scientifically, we can still appreciate the yogins' deep concern for how important respiration is for the human being. I might mention here that in Yoga there are similar approaches, such as the teaching of techniques that energize or re-charge the body and which combine breathing exercises with various physical exercises that are quite similar to Jacobson's Progressive Relaxation technique. This is particularly interesting since other therapists, including myself, have found that Progressive Relaxation is more effective when the inhalation/exhalation is incorporated with the technique.

Points to remember and emphasize with clients:

Our breathing patterns are directly related to our general health, our energy levels, and our level of stress.

Breathing exercises can serve to increase the efficiency of the respiratory process, increase our energy, calm the body, and keep the mind more alert.

For complete and efficient use of the respiratory mechanism, we need to involve:

The diaphragm and upper abdomen

The mid-thoracic

The upper thoracic or clavicle area

All three should be engaged during the respiratory cycle.

For the therapist, there are four issues to consider when working to achieve proper breathing:

The rate of breathing

The volume of air inhaled or exhaled

The utilization of the entire breathing apparatus

The rhythm of breathing over time, which includes noting problems like breath holding, frequent sighing, irregular cycles, etc.

To help you in deciding what breathing exercises to prescribe, here are some guidelines:

Have the clients put one hand on their chest and the other hand on their abdomen.

Observe their normal breathing patterns for any problems. Are they doing 3-stage breathing? In other words, are they breathing evenly into the abdomen, mid-chest, and upper chest (clavicle area).

Is the client breathing rhythmically (following the same steady in and out motion over time or does it shift)

Do they sigh frequently or hold the breath?

When talking, do they take extremely shallow, quick inhalations? (rapid speech may be an indication.)

Also use previous evaluations to help you. For example, any chronic anxiety-related symptom usually indicates poor diaphragmatic breathing and frequent holding of the breath, especially during times of stress.

Diaphragmatic Breathing

Lying on a bed, couch, or in a comfortable chair, place your right hand on your upper abdomen, with the palm of your hand resting just above your navel. Place your left hand on the upper chest. As you breathe, allow the air to move down into the abdomen (as if you were filling your stomach with air). The right hand should rise with the inhalation and fall with the exhalation; the left hand should move very little in this first phase. Do not try to force the movement; it should be gently encouraged only. Practice for 10 or more minutes, at least two times per day, such as when you go to bed and just before getting up in the morning. If you find difficulty with this exercise after a few days of practice, shift to using only your imagination, imaging the correct process without making any conscious effort; this often helps to encourage the necessary change.

Benefits: This exercise leads to better autonomic nervous system balance, greater relaxation, a greater efficiency of the pulmonary process, and reduces the amount of work needed for proper respiration. Anxiety related symptoms are particularly helped, along with general pulmonary problems like asthma.

Complete Breathing: Three-Stage Breathing

Once you're able to do diaphragmatic breathing with no difficulty, and find yourself breathing this way during the day, then you are ready to learn this exercise. In this exercise, all three mechanisms of breathing (diaphragmatic, mid, and upper thoracic) are brought into use. Inhale first, feeling the air expanding down into the diaphragm and expanding the belly, much like blowing up a balloon, where the end of the balloon expands first. Then continue the inhalation by expanding the mid chest; then let the inhalation continue to the very top of the lungs at which point a slight upward movement of the clavicles is experienced.

The exhalation is done in reverse motion, letting the clavicles drop slightly, then letting the chest collapse, and letting the belly collapse as the diaphragm moves upward, pushing air out of the lungs. Practice for 10 or more minutes. This exercise is best done either standing or sitting in a straight-backed chair, leaning just slightly forward. When the spine is straight and the chest and abdomen relaxed, this type of breathing should be automatic. The goal is to experience it without any effort, just allowing the body to breathe naturally. Again, use your imagination to help the body make the necessary corrections. Remember that correct breathing is efficient breathing, using far less energy than you currently use. If there is any extra effort in learning these new breathing patterns, then it means that you are trying too hard.

> **Benefits:** The same as "diaphragmatic breathing," except that this exercise is the final goal in correct breathing and is therefore the most effective and most energy efficient.

Quick Breath

Perform this exercise while standing or while sitting on the edge of a firm chair. Bring your awareness to your breathing and establish the "complete breath." Now inhale slowly and evenly through your nostrils, allowing your diaphragm and lungs to be fully extended; then in a single movement, push all the air out through your mouth by pulling your abdominal muscles in and up forcefully. The outgoing breath will make a "huh" sound. Continue this sequence for 12 to 15 breaths, or until you begin to feel dizzy. Rest until the dizziness disappears. This is one round. Start with four rounds. Your ability to progress will be judged by your measure of dizziness. As you continue to practice, you will be able to expand the number of breaths before feeling dizzy. Check with the therapist before increasing.

> Caution: This exercise should only be practiced on an empty stomach or 2 to 3 hours after eating.
>
> **Benefits:** This is an excellent exercise for aerobic stimulation and improving one's energy level. This is especially helpful for those clients who cannot perform aerobic exercise because of a disability, etc., or for clients who simply do not maintain a regular exercise program. It is also helpful for those with bronchial congestion, such as a cold or flu (making variations such as doing it for much shorter lengths of time, but more frequently). A congested nose is usually not a deterrent because one can usually force the air through with a little effort and this process helps to reduce mucous in the bronchial passages. In general, breathing exercises can help speed up healing because of the increase in energy one receives. The important point is to not tire the body by overdoing the exercise, since this might negate its benefits.

Ratio Breathing During Exercise

This special breathing is to be done while performing aerobic exercise such as walking, jogging, bicycling, using a rowing machine, etc, where the movements are performed the same way over and over again. This exercise correlates the rhythm of the breathing with movements of the body. Let's use walking as an example: Start with a ratio of 4:6, which means taking four steps as you inhale and six steps as you exhale, keeping this ratio constant as you are walking along. You will need to keep your focus on your breathing and your walking, which is desirable anyway. If you are walking very fast or if you begin to tire, you may find a 4:4 ratio more suitable. After a 2 to 4 weeks of regular practice, stretching your lung capacity by increasing the ratio to 6:8 or 6:10. Feel free to develop the ratio that best suits you, since these are only general guidelines. The same sort of ratio can be developed for jogging, bicycling, etc. As you begin to tire, you will likely need to adjust the ratio to a more even and shorter ratio.

> **Benefits:** This exercise is excellent for teaching your body to breath in a more naturally rhythmic pattern, a problem from which many people suffer. It is also excellent for increasing lung capacity and aerobic endurance because you are forcing the lungs to work harder by using a ratio and increasing it as you progress. Additionally, it tends to create more aerobic stimulation in a much shorter time. Even a 10-minute walk can be invigorating with an extended ratio. Lastly, it keeps the concentration on the breath and body, which is where it should be during exercise. This in turn, increases general concentration abilities, as well as training you to be more sensitive to the body.

Review of Stretching and Breathing Exercises
Review Practice:
- Frequency of practice
- Time and place of practice
- Experiences from practice
- Involve client in a general discussion of their practice and address any issues that arise
- Address resistances to daily practice
- Be prepared with rationales for home practice

Breathing Exercise:
- Check to be sure exercise is being done correctly
- Have client demonstrate
- If you notice problems, have client practice in front of you until they are consistent

Emphasize:

- Diaphragmatic breathing is one of the quickest ways to induce a state of relaxation
- Chest breathing exclusively can induce a state of anxiety
- Full breathing goes down into lower lobes of lungs where the exchange of blood and oxygen is richer
- Correct breathing helps eliminate carbon dioxide from lungs.
- Incorrect breathing can cause fatigue.
- Check breathing frequently throughout day.
- Check how breathing changes with feelings.
- Begin breathing correctly when you check.
- Always practice for 5-10 minutes in bed upon awakening and before sleep
- You're breathing all day anyway, might as well do it correctly.

Stretching:
Emphasize:

- Want to make sure you're doing it correctly
- Want you to succeed and also not create more tension by doing it incorrectly
- Stretching helps you create a greater body awareness
- Increases flexibility so you are less likely to sustain Injuries.
- Promotes more relaxed muscles
- Decreases stiffness (flexible muscles do not accumulate lactic acid the way tense muscles do)

4

Progressive Relaxation

Purpose of this Chapter

Develop an introductory understanding of Progressive Relaxation

Understand how and why PR is used to help your clients

Develop a working knowledge of EMG Biofeedback

Understand how and why this type of biofeedback training can help clients

Progressive Relaxation

As was discussed in an earlier section, Progressive Relaxation was developed by Edmund Jacobson in the early to mid 1900's. His research arose from the belief that the social trend toward high nervous tension could result in various types of illnesses (1934/1962). Jacobson believed that this nervous tension was both mental and physical. Jacobson's research found that whenever there was nervous tension, there was always a contraction (shortening) of skeletal fibers. Further, he found that when these skeletal fibers were relaxed (lengthened), there was a reduction in nervous tension.

Hence, he discovered that nervous tension and muscular relaxation were incompatible states. This view was further validated by Joseph Wolpe (1958) in his development of systematic desensitization.

Further research by Jacobson also found:

1. People who have not developed the skill of muscular relaxation have less ability to control their stress.
2. Stress is responsible for a variety of health disorders.
3. The teaching of PR has proven to be useful for a variety of disorders, including hypertension, anxiety, phobias, insomnia, minor depression, headaches, colitis, ulcers, and chronic pain.

Since the neuromuscular system is fairly easy to monitor using the electromyograph (EMG), and because it is under voluntary control, it is an excellent bodily system to work with in developing deep relaxation. Through his research, Jacobson developed the training method, PR, to guide his patients toward tension control via muscular relaxation.

According to McGuigan (1981):

> In learning PR, we must cultivate sensitive observations of the internal sensory world equal to our natural ability to observe the external environment. In acquiring heightened internal sensory observation, one employs two simple, straightforward physiological principles: 1) learn to recognize a state of tension, and 2) relax that tension and contrast it with the state of relaxation. Each of the major muscle groups is then systematically tensed so that the learner can identify the unique tension sensation (control signal) for that muscle group. The tension is studied, then relaxed away.... The tension sensation is called "the control signal" because it is literally a control for neuromuscular circuits.... By learning internal sensory observation you can become quite proficient in recognizing ("observing") your control signals wherever they may occur throughout the skeletal musculature. The long range goal of PR is for the body to instantaneously monitor all of the control signals, and automatically relieve tensions that are not desired (pp. 31-32).

Although Jacobson was interested only in relaxation of the muscles, I want to add that this technique also serves to lightly tone muscles as well. There are, then, two benefits that are derived from this technique, although the focus here will be more on the relaxation benefit. PR involves the tensing and relaxation of 15 major muscle groups in the body. Jacobson (1934/1962) and McGuigan (1981) instructed clients to practice 50 minutes one time per day for a total of 56 training sessions. Other researchers and clinicians, such as Wolpe (1958) and Budzynski (1974), have developed modified PR (MPR) techniques aimed at a shorter training period. I have found the modified PR to be more practical as well.

Besides shortening the time of PR, another change in the technique for many clinicians has been the addition of breathing in a specified manner as one tenses and relaxes the muscles. I have found that breathing in as you tense the muscle and breathing out as you relax the muscle works best. As you inhale, your heart rate increases and you draw oxygen through the body and, at the same time, you are also tensing the muscles which stimulates and draws blood flow and oxygen to them. As you exhale, your heart rate slows and the body relaxes and, at the same time, you release the muscle tension and feel the muscle group relaxing. Its important to emphasize to the client to exhale for as long as possible to increase the relaxing feeling and to enjoy this very pleasant experience. This will serve to stimulate the memory, learning, and behavior related to this experience and speed up the client's skill at attaining the alert mind and calm body state. To guide you in the development of your own approach to PR, here is a script that you can record on CD. Aspects of the script are taken from various sources, such as Budzynski's MPR (1972). The muscle groups that are covered are:

CD: Side One: Shoulders, mid, and lower body

Right forearm (front muscle group)
Right forearm (back muscle group)
Left forearm (front muscle group)
Left forearm (back muscle group)
Right bicep
Left bicep
Chest and upper back
Abdomen
Lower back
Buttocks
Right front thigh
Right back thigh
Left front thigh
Left back thigh
Right calf
Left calf

CD: Side Two: Upper body, head, and face

Chest and upper back
Shoulders
Neck
Jaw
Tongue
Forehead and eyebrows
Eyes

As you can see, I have divided the MPR into two separate training periods. This gives you the flexibility of having clients practicing the CD at each practice session twice per day, each taking approximately 20 minutes, or practice both one time per day for an approximate 40 minute practice session. You can give your clients the option, depending on their schedules and preferences.

Key points to remember and emphasize with clients

- PR helps differentiate between a state of tension and state of relaxation.
- You are learning to determine and pinpoint particular areas in the body which are tense (muscle separation and discrimination). You can learn to control these muscle groups.
- PR involves tensing particular muscle groups in the body and then slowly relaxing these muscles.
- This is accomplished through active concentration on muscle groups.
- Concentration allows awareness of what muscles feel like when tense, when they are in gradual stages of relaxation or tension, and when they're completely relaxed.
- This awareness becomes habitual with practice (i.e., unconscious).
- Lower levels of tension then begin to trigger conscious awareness at times during the day. This is the goal.
- With practice, you will be able to quickly scan muscles with the mind and be able to relax any muscles that are tense.
- Each time you practice, spend more time in the experience of letting go and exhaling, enjoying this extremely pleasant feeling of calmness and tranquility for these brief seconds.
- Although tensing is always important for toning and stimulating muscles and giving us more energy, it's also important to practice letting the tension go without tensing. This demonstrates your skill at using volition alone to relax. Practice both approaches during the day as you scan muscles.
- The technique becomes more subtle over time and more mental because you are strengthening the neural pathways between the brain and each muscle group.
- Increased awareness of the muscles, ability to keep them strong and healthy, and the ability to bring them under the natural control of passive volition are the goals of PR. Some clients may also report needing less sleep because they are using less energy during the day and sleeping more soundly at night.

Explain training CD; in other words, the nature of the CD practice, along with the purpose and value of the practice.

Review of Modified PR

First review stretching/breathing exercises and modify exercises as needed. Review MPR:

- Is client practicing at home?
- How often?
- If client isn't practicing enough: Review importance of home practice (is a skill; more practice, faster skill acquired; why aren't they practicing?).
- Go through daily schedule-how can times be fit in?

To help encourage practice for shorter time periods, try a **Ten Minute MPR:**

Lie on back on bed or floor, small or no pillow; arms at your sides, feet slightly apart, no body limbs touching.

Tighten left arm as you inhale, hold, feel tension, relax as you exhale. Do right arm same way. Holding neck to the right as you inhale, feel tension, then relax while exhaling. Same to the left. Hold head back as you inhale, feel tension in back of neck; exhale and pull head down towards the chest as you inhale, feel tension in front of neck, relax as you exhale. Stretch shoulders up around ears as you inhale, feel tension, relax as you exhale. Repeat.

Tighten up chest muscles as you inhale, feel tension, relax as you exhale. Repeat. Tense abdominal muscles as you inhale, feel tension, relax as you exhale. Tense left leg, pulling toes back, tightening upper and lower leg as you inhale, feel tension, relax as you exhale. Do right leg same way. Scan body with mind's eye and tighten and relax any muscle that feels tight. Feel a general sense of relaxation in the body; feel the breathing coming in and going out slowly, naturally; get up when ready.

Continue to review MPR: Go through the rest of the client's schedule and try and get 1 to 2 other practice times set up (make sure they're at least one hour before bed, unless they have insomnia, then make one practice time at bedtime). For example: When you practice, where do you notice tension, soreness and/or numbness? Recommend body scanning during day and discuss generalization effects. Emphasize the use of skills during the day. Discuss importance of time between actual practice and returning to daily activities (slow return, exaggerated slow movements, etc.)

Electromyograph Biofeedback

Measures muscle tension and relaxation.
Very sensitive to tension levels.
Non-invasive (no discomfort involved).

How EMG was Developed

As scientific and technological progress continued in the 1920s, the application of the vacuum tube in the psychophysiology laboratory provided a major breakthrough in the measurement of tension. In collaboration with Bell Telephone Laboratories, Dr. Jacobson pioneered the field of quantitative electromyography. We know that when muscles contract (tense) an electrical signal is thereby generated. By placing a pair of electrodes over the muscle on the skin, that electrical signal can be sensed, directed into a set of amplifiers, recorded, and then scientifically studied.... With the guidance furnished by such objective measures of tension and relaxation, it was possible to develop Progressive Relaxation into an effective technique. (McGuigan, 1981, pp.44-45)

This was how the EMG came into being. Since this time, it has proven to be a real boon in medical and psychological research and practice. But it was not used as a biofeedback device until the 1950s. The early EMG instruments were not very flexible in the way they measured and fed back information and were not that accurate because of artifact, such as that caused by electrical interference or poor electrode contact with the skin. More sophisticated electronics with better signal-to-noise ratio, the use of band-pass filters, and high quality surface electrodes, has enabled the biofeedback industry to standardize their instruments and increase the accuracy of the measurements. And with the onset of microcomputers and biofeedback software, we have entered a new era of biofeedback capabilities.

Basic EMG Biofeedback Electronics

The biofeedback instrument needs to detect a clear signal from the muscle, which must be picked up through the skin by the surface electrodes, and then passed on to the instrument for processing. It is finally displayed to the client via meters, sounds, etc.

The electrical signal from the muscle has two dimensions:

1. The *amplitude* of the signal, measured in *microvolts*. This measurement tells us how strong the signal is and, therefore, indicates the degree of muscle contraction.

2. The *frequency range*, measured in *hertz*. This tells us the overall range of the signal. Because of other electrical signals that are often present, we can have interference with the EMG signal. This is referred to as *artifact*. Consequently, the frequency range is narrowed to a "safe" range where artifact is less likely to occur. This narrowing of the frequency range, or the complete suppression

of a range, is accomplished by the use of *filters*. For example, if the desired frequency range is from 100-200 Hz, then filters would be used to eliminate all frequencies below 100 Hz and above 200 Hz.

Another consideration in regard to the EMG signal has to do with how "clean" the signal is because there will always be a certain level of "noise" or interference that is picked up with the signal. We can think of this as a ratio between the signal and the noise level and is referred to as the *signal-to-noise ratio*. The ratio should be as high as possible and is measured in *decibels*. To make sure that the incoming signal is only what you want and not extraneous energy, three electrodes are used. Two of these electrodes are called *active* and the other is called the *reference* or *ground* electrode. The purpose of this design is to create two separate signals or "sources" coming into the EMG instrument. This is necessary so as to separate the EMG signal from other electrical signals.

While the reference electrode may be placed at various places on the body, it is typically placed between the two active electrodes. The instrument then subtracts the voltages at "source one" from "source two," with the remaining difference being amplified by what is called a *differential amplifier*. Many of the newer hardware have all three electrodes pre-wired within a single triadic sensor, which makes placement easier.

EMG Placement Sites and Skin Preparation

There are common sites that are used when doing EMG training. These are sites that are related to chronic bracing, injury, or disorders (dysponesis). The most common ones you will use are: Facial: Frontalis (forehead), masseter (jaw), temporal (temple area); Upper and Mid Back: Cervical (neck), Upper trapezius (top of shoulders, Mid-Trapezius (between shoulder blades); Lower back: Lower thoracic and lumbosacral regions. You can also monitor other sites as specific needs dictate. Additionally, you can initially train on the forearm for initial practice.

The electrodes must make sufficient contact with the skin to pick up a clean, strong signal. This is attained at least three ways:

An electrode gel or paste must be used. This is placed in the electrode disc. The disc is filled to surface edge; but if it is filled too full or too low with paste, it can cause insufficient contact with the skin.

The electrodes must be properly attached to the skin to prevent movement. This is typically achieved by the use of electrode adhesive collars which are double sided; one side attaches to the electrode insulator edge, the other side is attached to the skin.

The skin must be properly prepared. This is accomplished by thoroughly cleaning the skin to eliminate surface materials, such as old skin, oil, or make-up. Alcohol on a cotton gauze is rubbed across the skin a few times; the skin should have a slightly reddened color from this light abrasive action.

Dysponesis

For training purposes related to general stress, you will be most concerned with dysponesis, the physical bracing efforts. Through previous evaluations, you determine the common bracing patterns of the client and give a fair amount of attention to this in training.

An example of how this can be done quite effectively is to attach the electrodes (usually dual electrodes in symmetrical fashion) to the bracing area. Then engage the client in conversation while keeping the EMG measurements in full visual or auditory view. As he or she talks and moves about in his or her chair, these patterns will quickly begin to show themselves for you and the client to see. It is helpful at such times to have the client attempt to reduce the levels before continuing the conversation. You can also have the client pretend to be working at a desk or any other situation that is common to them and then observe the bracing patterns. Working with the EMG in this way comes as close as possible to measuring the client in natural, day-to-day action situations. This is "relaxation-in-action" and is very important for creating true change.

First Session Practice

Explain to client that you want them to practice in the session so that you can answer questions related to practice and so that you can monitor the biofeedback. Emphasize that they need not be concerned about the biofeedback in this session, but that you want to take some measurements while they practice.

Attach the EMG sensors to the forearm and have the client tense and relax to show how it works (see below for more information on EMG biofeedback). Turn sound feedback off. Have client get comfortable (recliner or comfortable chair is preferable).

Use headphones and dim the lights. Put on relaxation CD and tell client to just follow the instructions. You will answer any questions related to the instructions after they have finished.

Ask the client to be aware of how they feel now before they practice. After the practice of the CD, remove headphones and answer any questions. Give necessary feedback on what you observed during the practice. Reinforce home practice and ask exactly when and where they will be practicing.

Emphasize that the CD is temporary until he or she can eventually do the relaxation without it.

In Next Session, Explain EMG training to client:

- Myo means muscle: Electro-myo-graph is the graphing or measuring of the electrical signals in the muscle. This information is then fed back to the client and therapist.

- When the brain wants to tense a muscle, it sends a signal through the neural pathways to a particular muscle.
- A split second later, the muscle then tightens in response to this electrical signal.
- The more the muscle tightens, the more electricity that is being produced.
- The EMG simply picks up whatever level of electricity that is being produced by the muscle and measures it via the electrodes, and then shows the level through visual indicators such as meters or lights, or auditorally through beeps, clicks, etc.
- EMG is like a sophisticated mirror that mirrors back whatever is going on in the muscle and amplifying it in a way that helps a person to understand what is happening. So there is a direct relationship: The tighter the muscle, the higher the signal displayed by the EMG.
- Your role, of course, is to learn how to relax your muscles which will bring EMG levels down.
- The EMG instruments puts no electricity in you, but simply picks up whatever is being produced by your body and displays it as sound or visual feedback.

EMG Practice:
- Attach electrodes to forearm for initial practice.
- Have client practice for 15 minutes.
- Re-attach electrodes to frontalis and have client practice for 15 minutes.
- Sit with client during these times and guide them along, giving appropriate suggestions as needed.
- After practice review procedures with client and answer any questions.

Review of Previous Techniques
Review stretching and breathing exercises: Quiz client to make sure they're practicing daily and achieving desired results.
- Recommend that client spend 30-60 seconds many times daily checking and correcting breathing, stretching, muscle scanning and releasing.
- Recommend following mini-relaxation: Muscle scan; tense-relax; slow, deep breathing; positive affirmation (e.g., "I feel good when I relax).
- Mini-relaxation can be done in most situations not requiring full concentration.
- Review MPR: Is client experiencing increased awareness of muscles and tension levels?
- Emphasize brief tensing and then spend the most time on letting go and feeling the relaxation.
- Review home practice and address concerns.

EMG Training:

- Review EMG rationale with client while attaching electrodes and checking instrumentation functions.
- Explain to client purpose of this particular session (based on individual protocols).
- Have client practice 20-30 minutes. Make yourself available during the session to check progress, answer questions, and give input.
- At end of EMG training, go over progress with client to make sure he or she understands what happened, what is supposed to happen, and strategies that he or she used or could have used during training. Look for any positives that you can give to reinforce client toward training.

5

Autogenic Training

Purpose of this Chapter

Develop a working understanding of Autogenic Training

Understand how and why Autogenic Training can be used to help your clients

Develop a basic knowledge of Thermal Biofeedback

Understand how and why this biofeedback training can be helpful for clients

Autogenic Training

I would like to start this section with a quote by Luthe (1979), the founder of Autogenic Training:

> One of the most important assumptions of autogenic therapy is that nature has provided man with homeostatic mechanisms not only to regulate fluid and electrolyte balance, blood pressure, heart rate, wound healing and so on, but also to readjust more complicated functional disorders that are of a mental nature. In autogenic therapy the term homeostatic self-regulatory brain mechanisms is

often used. This concept assumes that when a person is exposed to excessive disturbing stimulation (either emotional or physical trauma), the brain has the potential to utilize natural biological processes to reduce the disturbing consequences of the stimulation (i.e., neutralization). At the mental level some of this self-regulatory neutralization or recuperation occurs naturally during sleep and dreams.... The techniques developed and used in autogenic therapy have been designed to support and facilitate the natural self-healing mechanisms that already exist. (p. 167)

As was mentioned earlier in chapter one, Autogenic means "self-generating," or "self-suggesting." The client generates the desired effects for him or herself through the use of prescribed verbal formula. Although the original Autogenic Training (AT) procedures involved a very long treatment program, more brief procedures have been developed, such as at the Menninger Foundation. While retaining the same verbal formula and sequence, these briefer versions are referred to as modified AT. Successful autogenic therapy is based on three main principles:

1. Mental repetition of a specific verbal formula for brief periods with each phrase taking 5-30 seconds and slowly increasing the time of each phrase up to 2-3 minutes.
2. Mental activity called "passive concentration."
3. Reduction of afferent stimulation.

The verbal formula consists of **six basic phrases** and two additional optional phrases that were proposed by Schultz and Luthe:

My arms are heavy
My arms are warm
My heartbeat is calm and regular
It breathes me, or, my breathing is slow and relaxed
My solar plexus is warm
My forehead is cool
My thoughts are clear and comfortable
I am at peace

The Autogenic phrases are quite powerful in their ability to affect change and to shift most clients to a deep state of relaxation. A major reason for the power of the verbal formula lies in its emphasis on calming and regulating the autonomic nervous system and corresponding emotional and mental patterns. Most experts in the field of psychophysiology consider the autonomic nervous system to be directly involved in stress. The overall experience of repeating the phrases produces a deep "letting go."

Where the Progressive Relaxation technique was one of active concentration and muscle activation, the Autogenic is more of a receptive concentration, having the mind alert and conscious, with no mental effort involved. You might explain to the client that this experience is similar to relaxing in a hot tub, or drifting off to sleep, except for one very important difference: The mind stays very aware of internal experiences and passively attends to what is going on. The experience of subtle internal processes during the Autogenic Training eventually becomes a vivid part of memory. With practice, the memories of these experiences become so strong and habitual that they find their way into the conscious mind during the day. Eventually, just remembering these experiences can bring about a more relaxed state of being. For the client, the practice effects should continue to deepen until the eight phrases are vividly experienced.

Once the practices begin, part of each session should be devoted to detailed questions by the therapist regarding these phrases and their accompanying sensations. If particular phrases do not evoke the desired experiences, have the client spend more time with those particular phrases, or have them add more imagery, etc., to enhance the sensations.

Shultz and Luthe also stated that, with practice, a particular low arousal state develops, a state they referred to as the **Autogenic Shift**. The Autogenic Shift takes place when the entire body, particularly from the neck down (the head should not experience warmth; we want to control the amount of blood flow to the head), becomes heavy, limp, and warm, with very little notice of unpleasant sensations in the body. The body is now deeply relaxed and in a state where self-healing can take place (i.e., homeostatic re-regulation) and the mind is clear and alert with excellent receptive concentration. The client will speak very favorably of this state (unless there are initial abreactions), finding it quite peaceful and tranquil. Often the client will say that he or she enjoys this state so much that there is no immediate desire to end it. This Autogenic Shift is a special state-dependent experience and appears to be synonymous with the alert mind and calm body state spoken of earlier.

Points to Remember and Emphasize with Clients:

- Autogenic means "self-generating" or "self-suggesting."
- Autogenic Training is a relaxation technique that has been used in hospitals and clinics in Europe and the U.S. for more than 70 years.
- AT is considered one of the most effective skills available for learning deep relaxation.
- Self-suggesting phrases which relate purely to relaxation are repeated within a person's mind while focusing attention on specific areas of the body.
- With practice, the body and emotions begin to respond to these mental suggestions.
- An example would be "my arms are heavy." You simply focus your mind on your arms while repeating the phrase "my arms are heavy" over and over in your mind.
- In time, the arms will begin to take on natural feelings of heaviness which indicate that the arms are beginning to relax and that concentration is improving.

- These phrases are more for the mind and emotions than for the body. The body already knows how to relax, how to feel heaviness, warmth, etc., in a natural way.
- It's the mind and emotions that get in the way and prevent the body from relaxing.
- Through concentration and mental suggestions, you are really teaching your mind and emotions how to support the body's natural desire to be relaxed.
- We're really just teaching mind, emotions, and body how to work together to enable you to live in a more healthy state.
- Other phrases such as: "my heartbeat is calm and regular" and "my breathing is slow and relaxed" are helping the various systems of the body to self-regulate at a healthy level.
- This technique requires a deep "letting go."
- Where the PR technique was one of active concentration and muscle activation, the autogenic technique requires more of a passive concentration, where the mind is alert and yet possesses a sense of flowing and letting go.
- Many of our autonomic responses require this in order to function properly; for example, swallowing, urinating, or when going to sleep. One has to let go and allow the experience to come about naturally.
- Ask the client if they have any questions about the technique.

An effective tool is to use a small hand-held thermometer. If you use them, tell clients that they are mini-biofeedback devices for monitoring their finger temperatures. I recommend that they tape it to their finger before practicing the Autogenic technique at home. They simply check their temperature before beginning training and then again when they are finished to see if the blood flow has increased to their hands. This enables them to have some direct feedback on their progress at home. Also recommend that clients do hand warming at other times when they are not listening to the CD. For example, when they are watching television, they can do hand warming during commercials, or at work, school, etc., they can practice during breaks. Clients who are motivated enough to do these "extra" practices tend to improve more quickly than other clients.

Another benefit to the use of the hand-held thermometers at home is that it helps to verify actual warming. In other words, in the early phases of training, clients will often not know if their hands are actually warming or if they are just imagining it. I tell them that it really doesn't matter early on since the imagery serves as a necessary "bridge" for actual warming and that the warming will come in due time. However, it is important for clients to have the feedback when the actual warming does occurs. This is usually reinforcing for clients and inspires them toward continuing.

Review of Autogenic Training

Review home practice of modified AT and any other techniques. Ask if there are any questions, and ask detailed questions of their experience with each phrase:

My arms are heavy

My legs are heavy

My breathing is slow and relaxed

My arms/hands are warm

My legs/feet are warm

My thoughts are clear and comfortable

My solar plexus is warm

My forehead is cool

My heartbeat is calm and regular

I am at peace

- Be sure to go through each phrase and ask them in detail what they are experiencing. If they are having any problems, suggest use of imagery to help them experience particular sensations (give suggestions; i.e., for heaviness: the arms and legs are bags of sand; sinking into the chair; for warmth, lying on the beach, relaxing in a hot tub).
- Review importance of autogenic phrases on producing deep relaxation.

Thermal (Blood Flow) Biofeedback

Thermal or skin temperature biofeedback is designed to measure and display changes in skin temperature from a selected site. Skin temperature is controlled by blood flow and is an autonomic response. So thermal biofeedback is designed to measure peripheral blood flow to the extremities (arms/hands and legs/feet). The electronic design of this biofeedback instrument is quite simple: It is really just a highly sensitive thermometer with the addition of visual and auditory feedback signals.

The reason for the use of thermal biofeedback as a training tool is because peripheral blood flow is extremely sensitive to stress. It is very reactive to sympathetic nervous system response, causing the tiny blood vessels in the extremities to contract (called vasoconstriction) and preventing sufficient blood flow from occurring. The body is designed by nature to constrict blood flow to the extremities as a survival mechanism. This is part of the well known "fight or flight" response that occurs during stress and can be either internally or externally stimulated. For example, the hands and feet can become quite cold when the environmental temperature is low. At such times, the blood is restricted to the head and trunk areas, where the major organs of the body are kept warm and in sufficient supply of blood. This same stress response, however, should not occur in a warm environment or after a person has come in from a cold environment and has had a half hour or so to warm up.

I often hear people, especially older folks, remark that they have "poor circulation" and that is why their hands and feet are frequently cold. But most poor circulation problems, like most (90%) of high blood pressure cases, do not have a known medical etiology; in other words, there is no known reason why most people have vasoconstriction problems. Consequently, we need to consider other factors that may be involved, like homeostatic dysregulation.

Thermal biofeedback is an excellent way to teach vasodilation to clients, particularly as part of an overall biofeedback/stress management program. When clients are sufficiently relaxed, vasodilation tends to occur automatically. Keep in mind that relaxation includes all mind-body systems, including the cardiovascular system. When a client states that they are very relaxed, but their hands are still cool, this clearly indicates that their cardiovascular system is not sufficiently relaxed. This system is very difficult for most clients to sense and so they will not be aware of the tension. But, with further training, such awareness should occur.

I might add that besides emotional stress, other physiological stresses, such as consumption of caffeine (and other drugs) and a lack of exercise can cause vasoconstriction. Regular exercise is extremely beneficial to the cardiovascular system and is very helpful for stimulating blood flow. This is one reason why many older people who do not exercise have circulation problems.

Thermal Biofeedback Training Considerations

- The room in which thermal training takes place should be kept between 70 and 74 degrees to prevent natural vasoconstriction. You can use your thermal biofeedback to measure the room temperature by keeping the sensor in a fixed position with plenty of space around it for a few minutes.
- Be aware of air vents, particularly air conditioning, that might blow directly on the client.
- Wait 5-10 minutes after the client has entered the room before attaching the sensor. This will give your client sufficient time to adjust to the new room temperature.
- When attaching the thermal sensor to the hands, use the end of the forefinger or middle finger, and attach the sensor to the back of the finger, near but not on, the nail. This position best prevents interference due to contact with other fingers or body areas. Have the client rest the hands on the arms of the chair, or on his or her lap with the palms facing upward and the hands not touching each other.
- Hand temperature can range from the 60 degree range to a high of 95.5 degrees. The goal is control or self-regulation of the blood flow, so keep in mind that unless the temperature is already at the highest level, the client is to practice raising it higher.
- Be aware that just because a client's hand temperature may be high in the session does not mean that it is this way all the time. Hand temperature can vary significantly, depending on moods, thoughts, the environment, etc.
- If clients do not carry a hand-held thermometer with them, have them check their temperature during the day by touching the fingers to the sides of the neck. If it feels at all cool, then the hands are in some degree of vasoconstriction. Have them note such times (i.e., environment, situation, mood, etc.).
- The importance of how much the hand temperature increases depends on the individual's initial hand temperature and the actual temperature after training. Regardless of the number of degrees of temperature increase, you still want the client to achieve levels as close to 96 degrees as possible. This, however, is only a guideline and you have to always consider individual differences.
- Avoid having clients get overly concerned about actual temperature readings. Have them focus, instead, on the process of increasing the temperature and the corresponding subjective state. Clients should begin, at some point, to correlate the temperature with their level of relaxation.
- To begin training, attach the sensor to a finger on the dominant hand. This is because the dominant hand is usually a little easier to regulate. Once they achieve some degree of control, you can switch to the other hand and/or use two sensors, one for each hand.

- Start the training with a brief relaxation exercise (3-5 minutes) and then let them take over and continue to relax, using the autogenic phrases (and any other techniques previously learned).
- Clients often do better when their eyes are kept closed most of the time, particularly in the beginning. Have them open their eyes every so often to check their progress. Some clients, however, do better with their eyes open, so let them choose what feels most comfortable.
- As clients get better at the training, have them keep their eyes open more so they can learn to generalize the effects into daily living situations.
- Once the client progresses with the visual feedback, add auditory feedback to enhance their awareness of the temperature changes. Keep the auditory volume fairly low so he or she can hear it but is not bothered by it.
- Occasionally a client may experience plateaus during the session where the temperature will stabilize and they will have difficulty increasing the temperature. At this point, you may want them to try other relaxation procedures to add a variety of signaling for the client. You may also want to switch to another finger or hand (or foot) in the training. The above guidelines are fairly brief and are not intended as sufficient in-and-of themselves for conducting thermal training.

Review Skin Temperature Training Guidelines
- Goal of skin temperature training is to learn to increase at will temperature/peripheral blood flow voluntarily while maintaining a passive, yet alert mental state.
- Skin temperature biofeedback measures the amount of blood flow to an area of the body and corresponds to the temperature of the skin over that area.
- By developing the skill of increasing the warmth of hands or feet (i.e., blood flow), you can re-balance the blood flow in the body in general. This can, in turn, contribute to an improvement in other cardiovascular functions, such as heart rate and blood pressure.
- Temperature level of hands indicate the level of physical relaxation of the cardiovascular system. The higher the skin temperature, the deeper the physical relaxation in this system.
- Skin temperature training helps you become more sensitive to subtle internal states.
- You should attempt to discover and become familiar with particular internal feelings and emotional states associated with different hand/foot temperatures.
- The body responds to what the mind is focusing on. So the mind needs to be on calming, pleasant thoughts via relaxation training.

- During training, maintain a casual "let it happen" attitude. Think, "I'll let it happen" as opposed to "I'll make it happen." Alert mind and calm body is what you want to keep in mind.
- Use imagery, particularly autogenic phrases and any others that you may find helpful. Discover which imagery mode–visual, auditory, or kinesthetic you work best in. This is the "door" into gaining control and relaxing. Remember: true control is a flexible attention and volition, whether receptive or active, according to your needs at that moment.
- Learn to trust and listen to your body and discover what it needs for relaxation.

Skin Temperature Training:

- Start with a 15 minute session.
- Sit with client during training and talk them through a brief relaxation sequence. Then observe the biofeedback as they practice, noting changes every 30-60 seconds.
- If they are having difficulties, guide them through another relaxation, using imagery that will correspond to warmth and heaviness.
- After training period, review with client how they did and ask them the methods (imagery, etc.) that were used.
- Have client begin another 15 minute training. Change the task somewhat to reduce boredom. For example, you can have them imagine a stressful situation while maintaining a good temperature level. Or have them shift from stressful scenes to relaxation ones and observe temperature differences. Note what effects these tasks had for client.
- After the second training period, again review it with the client.
- Reinforce any positive training results and give encouragement for future success.

6

Therapeutic Imagery Training

The Purpose of this Chapter

Understand what therapeutic imagery is and how it is used

Become familiar with the different ways to use imagery

Help clients enhance their ability to use imagery for healing and change

Teach clients Imagery Enhancement Training

Learn how to use Imagery Desensitization with your clients

Therapeutic Imagery Training

The application of imagery techniques to psychotherapy evolved from two general influences: European methods and methods developed in the U.S. (Singer, 1974). In Europe, Desoilles, Leuner, Assagioli, and Schultz are credited with the development of imagery methods. They saw imagery as the direct voice of the unconscious, rather than as a defense against the impulse. This emphasis on imagery broke from the more traditional psychoanalytic view, where Freud saw imagery as simply what a memory concealed.

In the U.S., Wolpe, Hammer, and the gestalt therapists are credited with the early development of imagery as a training tool. Within behaviorism, imagery was first ignored because it was an internal process and not available for overt conditioning. It was Wolpe who changed all that with his investigation of covert processes and his development of systematic desensitization (Wolpe, 1958). Covert conditioning has now become an acceptable component of behaviorism and many of the procedures involve the contingent use of imagery (Cautela & McCullough, 1978). Also in the U.S., the gestalt therapists found imagery to be extremely beneficial in getting clients more in touch with their feelings.

I personally have found that all of these approaches to imagery have validity and usefulness. Psychodynamically, it seems that imagery does, indeed, enable the therapist to get at the unconscious quickly and effectively. It seems that one of the outstanding benefits is its ability to circumvent resistance by going directly to the unconscious rather than through the ego structures as in traditional psychodynamic therapy. Additionally, because of the therapeutic approach, transference isn't a dominant factor, although it will still occur to a lesser degree, depending on your overall therapeutic relationship and clinical approaches with your client.

Moving to the behavioral perspective, we find an avoidance of psychodynamic explanations, but the behaviorists have found that covert conditioning using imagery can be effective. Systematic desensitization has been well validated as an important approach to phobias and other anxiety-based disorders. In addition, the behaviorists have contributed in the area of teaching clients how to improve their imagery capacity and in making images more vivid and more controllable (Cautela & McCullough, 1978).

In the training procedures up to this point, the emphasis has been more on relaxation and biofeedback. This, of course, does not mean that imagery has not been used, because one could not learn to relax without imagery. PR and breathing make use of kinesthetic images; AT makes use of kinesthetic and visual images; and the concentration techniques make use of visual, auditory, and kinesthetic images. It is somewhat arbitrary to try and separate imagery from these other procedures, except for theoretical understanding.

There is also another rationale for proceeding in this manner: Relaxation is an excellent prerequisite for imagery training. Support in the literature shows that most imagery training relies on relaxation, at least initially. Recent research has also found that relaxation doesn't necessarily produce positive affect and imagery, as might be assumed with such methods as systematic desensitization. Instead, relaxation can help increase the experience of affect or imagery more vividly, thus helping a client directly face his or her issues rather than avoiding them and, in this way, learn to work through them. I might add that I personally believe that imagery is also greatly enhanced through active-receptive concentration techniques. For example, Cautela and McCullough (1978) describe an imagery technique:

> In imagery training, the client is instructed to look at various objects in the office, close his eyes, and describe the object. This is repeated until the client is able to give a fairly accurate and detailed description of a newly presented object... (p. 237)

This technique is hardly new and techniques like this one have been used for centuries in helping people enhance their concentration. Such techniques are frequently used by sports psychologists in helping athletes keep their mind focused. But Cautela and McCullough are also correct in prescribing such a technique for imagery training, because as one's concentration improves with this type of technique, one's ability to image is automatically enhanced.

Our shift to the more direct use of imagery is really a subtle, yet important one. This phase of the training serves at least three purposes:

- It will help clients learn to image more vividly and better control their images.
- Clients will also practice replacing negative images with positive ones (this includes, of course, other cognitive strategies) in dealing with phobias, anxiety, and related issues.
- This phase will also serve as an excellent preparation for some of the more advanced imagery procedures.

Points to Remember:

Imagery evolved from European methods where it was used to explore the subconscious; from the U.S. where it was used by the Gestalt therapists for helping clients get in better touch with their feelings; and from the behaviorists where it has been used for covert conditioning.

Imagery has particular appeal for those working with psychodynamic issues because it tends to circumvent resistance as well as put less emphasis on transference issues; this serves to greatly shorten the time needed to make therapeutic gain.

Imagery is an integral part of all relaxation and biofeedback training and cannot really be separated from them except for discussion purposes.

Relaxation not only helps a client to image more effectively, but also helps in getting in touch with those images that are emotionally charged. Hence relaxation has three benefits: To help stimulate active and receptive images; to be able to shift from negative images to more positive ones; and to help make negative images more vivid. This is discussed in more detail in the section, "Imagery Desensitization."

Imagery Enhancement Training (IET)

The following is a series of techniques that will help clients strengthen three abilities: To image at will, to enhance the vividness of an image, and to change the image as desired. Because IET follows the development of relaxation and concentration skills, you will find that most clients will proceed through this phase of the program with little difficulty. IET will form a natural and necessary bridge for the next technique, "Imagery Desensitization," a modified systematic desensitization technique, and for the advanced imagery techniques.

IET presents clients with a series of images. The images are not only visual, but also auditory and kinesthetic. The client is asked to image an object, scene, feeling, etc., and to be there with that image; in other words, feel that he or she is totally experiencing the image, not just seeing or hearing it. This will enhance the vividness of the image. Additionally, the client is instructed to either hold the image the same way for a designated time, or to start with an image and then change it in a particular manner. This will help the client learn to regulate the image.

IET is also helpful in determining where a client is weak or strong in his or her imagery capacity. By having clients complete a brief questionnaire at the end of their practice sessions (home or clinic), you can review their experiences for information on where they may be having problems, as well as in which mode they are strong; use this information for future reference in working with them. For the actual IET script, see Appendix.

Points to Emphasize with Clients:

- IET will help to increase your imagery ability.
- You will learn to bring about any image, positive or negative, at will.
- You will also learn to experience an image as vividly as needed.
- You will practice holding images a certain way and learn to change the image as instructed.
- You will also learn how to get more deeply in touch with negative thoughts or feelings through imagery, how to change them to more positive ones, and how to use positive images to become more calm, attentive, problem-solve, or attain certain goals.
- Remember that relaxation is very important for imagery. Avoid strain and excessive effort.
- Just use your relaxation and concentration skills to practice the technique, not concerning yourself with how well you are doing.
- As you practice, you will notice the skills developing naturally according to your individual make-up.
- Notice what images seem to be easiest for you to imagine. Note this after each practice session for the therapist.

- Follow the instuctions on the CD and if you have any questions, ask the therapist. Its important that you fully understand how to do the practice, so don't hesitate in getting clarification.

After IET Practices:
- Review previous training.
- Review IET home practice
- Is client doing home practice?
- Frequency?
- Review with client the experiences with home practice. In other words, how are their imagery skills developing? Are the images becoming more vivid, more self-regulated with practice?
- What images are easiest for them? Most difficult?
- Give any suggestions that might help them where are they are experiencing difficulty.
- Recommend that they also practice at other times during the day, such as at work for very brief periods. For example, they can close their eyes and practice imaging certain objects, scenes, etc., making them as vivid as possible, as well as changing them at will.
- You can also have them image some object like a picture, pencil, etc., and then close their eyes and visualize the afterimage. They can do the same with the auditory and kinesthetic realm.
- Remember: This will strengthen concentration skills as well.

Imagery Desensitization Training (IDT)

The development of systematic desensitization by Wolpe was a very significant event in the history of psychotherapy for three reasons: It was the first time behavior modification was used for covert conditioning; it emphasized the important role of relaxation in reducing anxiety-related problems; and it demonstrated the use of imagery for the purpose of self-regulation.

Systematic desensitization is well supported by research studies for its use in phobias and anxiety-related disorders. However, various controversies have arisen concerning exactly why systematic desensitization works. At least three components of the method have been indicated as possible contributors to its effectiveness: Its matching of relaxation with anxiety, its use of imagery, and its use of the hierarchy construction. I want to cover each of these to help you better understand where the technique's effectiveness lies.

Wolpe asserts that his own method's effectiveness is because of reciprocal inhibition, there are research studies that show that this may not be what occurs. These studies have found that relaxation may not be the effective component in reducing the client's anxiety. In fact, it has been found that relaxation can actually intensify the person's experience of anxiety-laden issues. Yet, there is also a great deal of research that supports relaxation in its ability to reduce anxiety.

This seemingly contradictory research is, in fact, not contradictory at all. If you refer back to chapter two in the section, "Core Therapeutic Skills Attained by Client," you will find that both of these benefits of relaxation are addressed. In "Accessing the Subconscious," it is explained that relaxation has the dual benefit of calming the mind-body system, making access to the unconscious easier and, in addition, helping a client experience the unconscious material that presents itself in therapy. Further, it was pointed out that relaxation (in conjunction with attentional control) can be used to help a client shift from an experience that is too intense and return to an alert mind and calm body state. The above research simply supports this dual benefit of relaxation in its use as a self-regulatory skill.

Returning to systematic desensitization, it seems that the relaxation is used to help a client get more in touch with anxiety-producing events by allowing the subconscious imagery associated with the anxiety to present itself to consciousness (Chapman & Feather, 1971). This is extremely important because clients tend to avoid focusing on the actual anxiety-producing stimuli; in therapy, they need to do this in order to produce change (Singer & Pope, 1978). If the anxiety becomes too great, the client can again use the relaxation to willfully shift their attention away from the anxiety and begin to calm down. When they have calmed down sufficiently, they can again shift back to the images associated with the anxiety.

Singer and Pope (1978) state that the research supports the use of imagery as a key component of systematic desensitization. It is becoming more clear that the reason why this technique is effective is because, first, the client is required to face their anxiety-producing images and that subsequent repetition can help reduce its potency. Second, clients on their own, if not actively guided by the therapist, will tend to generate positive images which seem to provide new psychological responses to the previous anxiety-producing ones. There are psychologists, such as Lazarus and Ahsen, who have developed training approaches based on this understanding. We might think of the conscious positive imagery as a tool for the cognitive mind to use in learning to cope effectively. By combining it with the relaxation, we can see how change can be produced. This view is very similar to the use of cognitive restructuring approaches.

The use of hierarchical construction is only weakly supported by research. However, as some researchers have pointed out, hierarchy construction has many clinical advantages and, therefore, should be used (Singer & Pope, 1978).

In summary, this discussion further supports how relaxation and imagery are intricately connected and are juxtaposed in the client's use of self-regulation skills. I have called this approach "Imagery Desensitization Training" because, in my own work, I have modified Wolpe's technique, emphasizing the role of imagery in conjunction with relaxation. In addition, I have made effective use of EDG biofeedback as an integral component of the technique. I believe that the role of biofeedback has significant advantages over Wolpe's approach where the client signals when they are feeling stress. It is helpful to supplement the client's subjective sense with a more objective and probably more accurate and consistent approach that can be provided with the biofeedback.

Points to Remember:
- Imagery Desensitization Training (IDT) emphasizes the central role of imagery in desensitization.
- IDT is designed to reduce chronic anxiety related to specific stimuli.
- Relaxation and imagery work hand-in-hand to produce change. Briefly, this is achieved by relaxation which helps a client relax sufficiently so as to produce the passive imagery associated with the anxiety.
- Focusing on the imagery in a repetitious manner helps reduce its potency.
- Additionally, the client can be taught to produce positive images which relate to the development of effective coping strategies for the anxiety producing event. If, in this process, the anxiety becomes too strong, the client can shift away from the negative images and relax until the anxiety is reduced enough to proceed further.
- The previous training of relaxation, concentration, and imagery enhancement will greatly serve the client in achieving positive results in the IDT technique.

Imagery Desensitization Training Procedures
Wolpe's (1973) systematic desensitization consists of three general phases: (a) Training in muscle relaxation; (b) Construction of hierarchies of anxiety-producing stimuli; and (c) The counterpoising of relaxation with the hierarchy stimuli.

By the time the client reaches this part of the training program, he or she has completed basic relaxation skill training and has practiced IET.

The therapist needs to establish the hierarchy of anxiety-producing stimuli. This is achieved much the same way as proposed by Wolpe. You can also use any number of anxiety or fear scales.

Next, explain to the client in detail the nature and components of a hierarchy. Give him or her examples as a guide.

A hierarchy is then created with the client.

The client is to rank the hierarchy from the least anxiety-producing to the most and to rate them from 0, being no anxiety, to 100, being the most anxiety-producing, similar to Wolpe's SUD ("Subjective Units of Disturbance").

The hierarchy construction is "put to the test" in determining the relevance of the various stimuli via the biofeedback monitoring. This addition to the SUD use is unique; it is not found in Wolpe's systematic desensitization. It appears, however, to be an essential component to determine what is truly relevant stimuli, as well as the place in the hierarchy. This is where the biofeedback is extremely valuable. In this phase, the client is monitored by the biofeedback, preferably the EDG or heart rate variability biofeedback.

The client is then given instructions to self-induce a state of relaxation and to let the therapist know when he or she is ready. During this time, a baseline is established.

Have client image unrelated benign stimuli to further check baselines. This usually serves as a good adjustment time for the client and will help elucidate erroneous readings.

This is followed by taking the client through the hierarchy, starting from the least anxiety-producing to the highest. As the client is taken through the hierarchy, the biofeedback measurements are used to check the ranked anxiety-producing stimuli. Changes in the hierarchy will, in most cases, be made. In this way, the therapist can develop a more accurate and relevant hierarchy for the client.

In most cases I tend to favor an abbreviated hierarchy and find that it can work equally well to an elaborate one. With the use of stimuli quantification with biofeedback, you can get a pretty good idea of the most relevant stimuli that are related to the client's problem and can focus in on the most essential stimuli.

Once the hierarchy is quantified, the client proceeds to the final phase. There are a large number of techniques and methods in this manual that can be taught at this phase beginning with Wolpe's own strategies.

More Advanced Imagery Training
A. Psychodynamic Imagery Strategy

This clinical approach is based on an integration of self-regulation concepts and the traditional psychodynamic view of traumas and other subconscious stress patterns. The goal here is to work with these dysfunctional patterns so as to help the client resolve them. This, of course, involves approaching the subconscious realm where the emotional stresses have been dissociated from the conscious mind.

At this primary level, these emotional stresses consist of images. Consequently, it is these images that need to be changed or resolved. Traditionally, one way to do this is by allowing the client to bring these images up spontaneously so that they can be resolved. This is free association. This technique, however, tends to be very slow and also triggers the ego's defense mechanisms. By using relaxation and imagery instead of free association, these primary images can surface more quickly and without resistance on the client's part.

Caution: This process is extremely effective, so one has to be very careful not to bring up too much too quickly. It is better to start with more benign images and to slowly proceed to more anxiety-producing images, although this is somewhat of a trial-and-error process. Here, the use of EDG or heart rate biofeedback is very helpful for monitoring the anxiety levels. I would highly recommend becoming familiar with standardized strategies, such as Hans Leuner's *Guided Affective Imagery*, as well as other imagery methods first before proceeding with this approach.

The therapist usually needs to make some suggestions, particularly in the beginning, to stimulate therapeutic movement. These suggestions are in the form of images or questions. For example, the therapist may use a standard setting such as a meadow to start the process and then add other standard images as needed to help the client get in touch with his or her conflict or anxiety. The therapist also needs to keep asking the client to describe what is happening so that the two are together with the experience. The role of the therapist should be seen as a gentle encourager, simply setting the therapeutic context as is needed and then backing off and letting the client's own processes take over. This usually isn't easy for the client which is why relaxation, concentration, and imagery training is so important as a prerequisite for this method.

A key consideration here is in not relying on therapist interpretations or solutions (although there will be some need for this at times), but more on clients arriving at their own solutions with your support and guidance. In this way, the solutions are usually more relevant to the client's particular idiosyncratic issues and tend to stimulate greater self-regulation. These solutions are often not obvious in terms of actual memory experiences. Instead, they usually occur as symbolic images that contain subconscious conflict, as least initially. As the client begins to work through them, oftentimes actual memories begin to surface, although this is not necessary for change. The client is then asked to confront, attempt to understand, and then resolve these symbolic images. There are many excellent techniques for doing this which I won't go into here. This resolution can be handled, if desired, in a fairly traditional psychodynamic manner, or based on other therapeutic orientations.

B. Accessing the Creative Subconscious

This approach goes beyond resolving conflicts and is more focused on the positive use of imagery for self-growth. I use this approach for conscious problem-solving and goal-setting. For example, when setting long-term goals, we want the clients to take charge of their creative mind and to arrive at the solution. We do not want the therapist to try and come up with solutions; but, we also don't want the client's own rational mind to take over. We might think of the creative mind as a temporary integration of rational and emotional factors that lead to insight and intuition. In this case, it is applied to goals or other personal needs that the client wants to resolve. This is also an emphasis on metacognition.

The strategy begins by explaining to the client ahead of time that they are to rely upon their creative insightful mind, which occurs spontaneously and without effort, using receptive attention and allowing images, ideas, and feelings which relate to solutions to occur naturally. Because of the Imagery Enhancement Training and the relaxation training, the client can more readily relate to and accept this approach to training.

Clients will oftentimes feel that they are "making up" such images or ideas that spontaneously arises. It is explained that this is natural and that it is not possible to tell where the images are coming from, but to continue with the process anyway.

One issue the therapist should be aware of is the tendency for the client to use their more logical or rational mind to give solutions during the imagery process. This is especially common if the client is having trouble with the process and feel they need to help or push the process along. Often, they are not even be to try and come up with solutions. aware they are doing this. So the therapist has to be very sensitive to this possibility. This is sometimes missed because the therapist's own logical, rational mind responds to the client's rational mind and so the therapist loses his/her objectivity to the process. An aspect of the rational mind is the tendency to evaluate and give logical meaning to what is occurring. While this is natural, the client is encouraged to be aware of this tendency so it doesn't interfere with the process.

With this imagery technique, it is helpful to use some suggestive images to start the process for the client. There are various approaches which can be used. For example, I sometimes use the Erickson and Rossi "Incubation Technique" (Rossi, 1988) or a variation of it. Sometimes solutions are elicited during the session and sometimes outside the session. The idea is to stimulate the creative mind in providing solutions which were previously unavailable. Clients will need varying amounts of imagery support and suggestions to help get the process going. One approach is to encourage the client to "brain storm" some ideas as a way of initiating the process; this helps the client to become more spontaneous and stimulate solutions. Again, this is different from a pure rational way of problem solving, but an attempt to pull from the client's own creative unconscious.

Remember: The symbols and metaphors of the client are idiosyncratic and, therefore, you are teaching the client the initial process of interpretation and working with their personal subconscious. Jung's archetypal theory and other well known approaches may be consulted for more information on this topic area.

Electrodermagraph Biofeedback

Our skin is the body's largest organ and is highly reactive to internal and external stimuli. Changes in emotional experiences have an almost immediate and measurable response within the skin. One of the changes is an increase or decrease in sweat gland activity. An increase accompanies general sympathetic arousal levels. Sweat gland activity has also been shown to be a good indicator of the orienting reflex, or what is also referred to as active attention. Since the 1800's, researchers have recorded changes in sweat gland activity using the galvanic skin response (GSR). In the early part of the 1900s, for example, psychiatrist Carl Jung used the GSR with clients to observe subconscious emotional responses to a word list. And the lie detector used by law enforcement is a type of GSR used to detect anxiety responses of suspected criminals.

Despite its long history and usefulness, the GSR has not had the kind of clinical research enjoyed by other biofeedback modalities. Such research is greatly needed to validate and clarify how it can be used to enhance self-regulation. Although we can consider ourselves within the early phases of GSR research, I believe we can still benefit from what we presently know. There are at least 10 terms used to describe sweat gland measurement. Electrodermagraph (EDG) is considered the general term to describe all of the different measurement techniques and instruments and is the term used here.

There are two different ways to measure electrodermal activity. In one, a current is passed through the skin and the resistance to the current is measured. In the other, no current is used and the skin is the source of electrical activity. The former approach is the most commonly used in clinical biofeedback. This approach is based on the understanding that as the sweat gland activity of the skin increases, the resistance (i.e., preventing the flow of an electrical current) decreases. Increased moisture heightens the electrical conductance, allowing the current to flow between two points on the skin When the person relaxes and decreases the sweat gland activity, the conductance decreases. Thus we can describe the EDG as measuring the electrical resistance of the skin. Actually, though, for measurement purposes, most psychotherapists use skin conductance, which is the reciprocal of skin resistance.

Measuring Phasic and Tonic Responses:

The EDG signal has two different signal responses. One component measures slow changes that take place over time and seem to correspond to non-directed activation. This is often referred to as the **tonic level**. The other component measures quick, transient changes in response to some stimuli; this often referred to as the **phasic level**. It is difficult to measure both tonic and phasic levels simultaneously, so two different displays or settings are often used. A common electronic design approach is to use a high-pass frequency filter to measure the phasic level and to show changes in the tonic level from an arbitrary zero point. This provides the necessary sensitivity to small changes within the usable range of the EDG. This type of design is effective for the kind of biofeedback training described in this manual.

Most EDG instruments use the same electrode design as was previously described for EMG biofeedback; in other words, a silver/silver chloride surface area and the use of an electrode paste.

Electrodermal Biofeedback Training Considerations

The electrodermagraph: derma means skin, hence the EDG measures the electrical activity of the skin produced by the sweat gland activity.

- Sweat gland activity is a response of the autonomic nervous system and is one indication of the arousal level of the person.
- EDG is a good measure of anxiety. Anxiety is usually triggered by various negative thoughts such as having to perform and the anticipation of an event or other mental projections which are perceived as potentially threatening.
- Anxiety is accompanied by particular negative images. These images are often very subtle and fleeting and may be difficult to detect.
- By learning to replace these negative images with positive ones, we can learn to control these anxiety responses.
- A part of EDG training is in learning to be more aware of the kinds of images that go through our mind and their effects upon us.
- With practice, you will be more aware of such negative images and how they trigger anxiety and other negative emotional responses. Learning to replace these negative images with positive ones will bring about positive inner changes.
- The EDG is extremely sensitive and quickly responds to the slightest shift in thoughts and feelings. It may also react strongly to breathing, movement, etc., too, so be aware of this during your practice.
- The electrodes are attached where the sweat gland activity is especially responsive to emotional reactions. This is usually the hands, particularly the finger tips (where the pad is) and the palms. If you attach the electrodes to the finger tips, avoid putting them next to each other since this can cause possible contact and shorting. I usually use the forefinger and ring finger. On the palm, I usually attach them at least one inch apart. No special preparation of the skin is necessary other than the hands being clean and free of excessive oils (including hand cream).
- There is a slight lapse between a physical response and its measurement showing on the EDG. It also takes several seconds for transient responses to return to the original levels.

- EDG responses are extremely responsive to variables such as coughing, movement, temperature, humidity, age, breathing, etc., so be aware of this when training.
- Upon initial electrode attachment, get some feel for a client's responsiveness by creating minor stresses and other variable responses through a series of mini-tests. For example, clap loudly near the client; have the client take a deep breath and hold it; have them shift in their chair and move their fingers; have them subtract numbers aloud, etc. Observe along with the client the EDG changes with each of these instructions, along with the overall level. This will begin to give you a good idea of the client's typical response patterns to daily situations. Is the client highly responsive? Is there almost no response? Does the EDG return to previous levels, or does it remain high? Explain to the client how such responses relate to effective coping.
- Consult your EDG instrument manual for the kinds of levels you should expect during training. This frequently varies according to the particular instrument and design.
- Low EDG levels do not necessarily mean relaxation. I have found that an extremely low response is often an indication of depression. It may also be encountered during counseling to indicate resistance.

EDG biofeedback is especially effective with imagery training. This is because imagery is subtle and very response to thoughts and feelings. We need an instrument that can measure this and respond quickly enough. The EDG is one biofeedback modality that can do this fairly effectively. Heart rate and EEG may also have some promise in this area and you may want to explore their use at some point. Remember that it is important to get to know the client's individual responsiveness with the EDG before using it as a clinical tool, such as in understanding his or her reaction to images or emotions.

Review of Electrodermal Biofeedback

- Measures very subtle changes in perspiration levels of the hands.
- Very sensitive to anxiety, thoughts, and feelings.
- Non-invasive (no discomfort).
- Let them know that you will explain EDG biofeedback more the next session, but you only want them to focus on the IET in this session, and to not be concerned with the biofeedback measurements.

In-session practice:

- Attach the electrodes (refer to them as sensors) to the client. Show them briefly how the EDG works. Then turn the biofeedback away from client for your own monitoring.

- Have client get comfortable.
- Use headphones.
- Dim lights.
- Put on IET CD and tell client to just follow the instructions. You will answer any questions related to the CD after he or she has finished.
- Ask client to be aware of how they feel right now before they start the practice.

After Listening to the CD:

- Remove headphones and answer any questions.
- Give necessary feedback on what you observed during the practice.
- Ask what his or her overall experience is after training.
- Reinforce role of home practice.
- Emphasize that the CD is temporary until he or she can learn to do the imagery without it.

Electrodermal Biofeedback Use in the Psychotherapy Setting

According to Fuller (1980) there are at least five different uses for EDG:

1. As a demonstration tool. The EDG is an excellent instrument for making the mind-body connection very clear. Besides with clients, I also often use it for lectures where I ask for a volunteer to demonstrate how it works. After attaching the electrodes and showing the audience the baseline response, I then ask for someone in the audience who knows the volunteer to ask him or her a personal and embarrassing question. Of course, I don't actually allow such a question to be asked, but there is almost always a dramatic EDG response to the anticipation of such a question. This anticipatory response is pointed out to the audience as a clear demonstration of a mind-body connection.

2. The characteristic patterns of response. Although not well researched thus far, many psychotherapists have noted that there appears to be a relationship of personality types and the kind of EDG responses that are measured.

3. For desensitization, as was previously discussed.

4. Lowering of sympathetic arousal. Conditions that are a direct result of, or that occur along with sympathetic arousal, can benefit from EDG training. In this training manual, this is accomplished through the relaxation training aspect of the program.

5. Exploration in psychotherapy. EDG can be used along with other non-verbal or psychophysiological cues in exploring deeper emotional issues. It is particularly helpful when using imagery and hypnosis.

In this chapter, the use of EDG is focused mostly on Imagery Enhancement Training and Imagery Desensitization. As you work with clients on imagery enhancement, you can note the kinds of reactivity that occurs. This helps you in understanding their individual response patterns which is essential for individualized approaches, such as in imagery desensitization.

EDG Practice:

- Attach sensors to client's hand, using either the fingers or palm.
- Take a baseline reading. Now refer back to "EDG Biofeedback Training Considerations" by taking the client through the series of mini-tests to check the client's reactivity. Take note of these responses for use in training. Discuss them with the client and what they mean. This information may be used in conjunction with information derived from a stress profile, or other assessments taken during the intake.
- Use the mini-test results and results from the assessment to structure EDG training in the session, having the client practice working with the EDG according to your instructions.
- Have client practice 20 to 30 minutes, guiding them along as needed. You may even want to leave them alone for a period of time if they are uncomfortable with your presence while they practice.
- After practice, review how they did and give appropriate feedback and suggestions.
- Review home practice guidelines as needed.

7

The Heart of Emotions: Heart Rate Variability Biofeedback

The Purpose of this Chapter

The role of the autonomic nervous system and heart rate and stress

Understanding heart rate variability and coherence

The role of respiration and heart rate coherence

Protocols for improving heart rate variability

Heart Rate Variability Biofeedback

One overall premise and guiding principle espoused in this manual is that we need to consider mind and body as one system. Physiological and psychological responses occur together, or closely follow one another. In addition to this view, we are moving away from the view that brain functioning occurs only in the white and gray matter encased in the head. Instead, we have discovered that neurons are found in other areas of the body as well and correspond to the nerve plexi along the spine and their innervation in bodily organs.

Recently, the cardiac and cervical plexi have come under increasing investigation in understanding their relationship to the heart. We can think of these neuronal systems as forming a functional "heart brain," in which the heart communicates with and influences brain functioning. For example, research has confirmed that such chronic reactions as anxiety, anger, and worry can have dramatic affects on the heart, increasing the risk of cardiac disorders. We also are beginning to understand that positive emotions can improve cardiac health, sometimes in significant ways.

One of the more exciting possibilities for the use of technology in the counseling profession is its potential for providing us with a better glimpse of the internal workings of the human mind. While no instrument can tell us what a person is thinking or feeling, all of the biofeedback modalities help us better understand what is going on in our clients, whether it be the measurement of muscle tension (surface EMG), constriction of blood flow (Thermal), perspiration levels (EDG), heart rhythm (HRV), or brain waves (EEG).

In comparing EMG, EDG, thermal, and neurofeedback modalities, the EDG comes the closest to indicating actual emotions, in this case, anxiety. This is quite beneficial, as for example, in working with phobias and other anxiety-based disorders. The use of EDG is limited, however, to mostly the measurement of these anxiety levels. What has been missing until more recently is a biofeedback instrument that can measure bodily responses that can differentiate between negative emotions and positive emotions, and how these emotional responses correlate with positive body states. Heart rhythm biofeedback (HRVB) goes a long way toward answering this need.

What exactly is HRV and HRV biofeedback? To quote McCraty and Tomasino (2004):

> Heart rate variability (HRV) is a measure of the naturally occurring beat-to-beat changes in heart rate. The analysis of HRV, or heart rhythms, is a powerful, non-invasive measure of neurocardiac function that reflects heart-brain interactions and autonomic nervous system dynamics....A promising advancement in biofeedback technology is the recent development of HRV feedback system. In relation to other types of biofeedback systems, HRV feedback offers several unique advantages. First, HRV feedback reflects the activity of both the sympathetic and parasympathetic branches of the autonomic nervous system and synchronization between them, and thus provides a window into the dynamics of the system as a whole. ...

HRV dynamics are particularly sensitive to changes in emotional state, and that positive and negative emotions can be readily distinguished by changes in heart rhythm patterns which are independent of heart rate. Specifically, during the experience of negative emotions such as anger, frustration, or anxiety, heart rhythms become more erratic or disordered, indicating less synchronization in the reciprocal action between the parasympathetic and sympathetic branches of the autonomic nervous system. In contrast, sustained positive emotions, such as appreciation, love, or compassion, are associated with a highly ordered or *coherent* pattern in the heart rhythm, reflecting greater synchronization between the two branches of the autonomic nervous system.

Stressors, which can come from a multitude of sources, temporarily interrupt the balance between the sympathetic and parasympathetic systems. This is natural, allowing the ANS to return to homeostasis once the stressors end. What is not natural is when we develop habitual and chronic stress responses that prevent the ANS from maintaining homeostasis. The development of chronic stress patterns occur with most people to different degrees of severity and will also vary in its effects on the body due to genetics and temperament. For example, some will have chronic stress in the musculo-skeletal system, others in the digestive system, and still others in the cardio-vascular system. Other stress patterns can have more of a mental health effect, such as with post-traumatic stress disorder, attachment disorders, bipolar disorder, and ADHD.

Because heart rate variability is directly affected by the ANS, attaining coherence is related to keeping the ANS in balance. It is this balance which allows the heart to vary its rhythm and provides a fairly good mirror of the body's response to stressors. This supports the use of HRVB as an effective modality in reducing habitual stress responses.

The Role of Respiration in HRVB

Respiration is largely regulated by the cervical plexus, which also helps regulate heart rate. Respiration is the only major autonomic system that we naturally have direct control over whenever we choose. In primary hatha yoga texts dating back hundreds of years, for example, there is much emphasis placed on the regulation of breath, which is believed to help regulate many aspects of the mind-body system. More modern research has now confirmed at least some of what these ancient teachings have taught, including the significant role that breathing plays in relation to the ANS.

Breathing techniques are currently taught as part of all heart rhythm biofeedback training protocols. Some suggestions on how to use these protocols effectively are mentioned later.

Applications for HRVB

While there are many medical applications for HRVB (hypertension, diabetes, cardiac rehab, etc.), our focus here is on those applications that are either directly related to emotional disorders, or disorders that are highly reactive to stress. To date, research has provided at least some validation for the following disorders:

- Depression
- Anxiety
- ADHD
- Panic disorder
- PTSD
- Fibromyalgia
- Chronic fatigue
- Sleep disorders
- Chronic pain
- Asthma

As you can see, there are a large number of potential applications of HRVB for the mental health clinician and you will surely have the opportunity to try HRVB with a number of your clients.

Basic HRVB Instrumentation

The two ways that heart rate can be measured is either through the use of an electrocardiogram (ECG), or by using pulse wave recordings, in which a plethysmographic optical sensor detects pulse rate. Pulse wave recording is taken from either the earlobe or fingertip. Although ECG recordings produce less artifact (interference), pulse wave recording is fine for most applications and is much more convenient and less expensive.

The pulse wave sensors do not require electrode gel or other accessories. They simply attach to the earlobe or fingertip and recordings can begin immediately. Most software also has the capability to determine if the pulse wave signal is accurate before beginning a treatment session. So the initial attachment process is extremely simple and quick.

Regardless of the particular company's software, there will be some form of visual and auditory feedback. This may be in the form of graphs, changes in tones, beats, etc., which indicate the shifts in the HRV and includes an actual readout of quantitative changes. To increase client interest, there are also attractive visualizations, games, etc., to hold the client's attention and increase their motivation toward positive change. Most software also include different levels of difficulty to slowly shape the client to achieve more and more difficult skill levels.

During training, the client will know exactly what their level of ability is and the degree of change that is needed. This helps clients get a sense of where they are with the training and, with practice, will easily determine how they are doing in terms of successful progress.

Another important feature of available software is the ability to collect data of each session, as well as plot changes over time. This allows the therapist to be very accurate as to the client's progress so that changes can be noted and can be reviewed with the client.

HRVB Software Protocols

Each company that makes HRVB instruments have their own software and protocols for their particular instrument. Please refer to these protocols when designing a training program for your client. In the next section, I will discuss some general protocol issues and suggestions for enhancing existing software protocols.

Key Points to Remember and Emphasize with Your Clients

- Heart rate variability is a measure of changes in heart rate
- This variability reflects how the brain and heart interact
- The autonomic nervous system (ANS) needs to function like a balance beam to maintain healthy physical and emotional states
- HRVB helps us to get feedback on our emotions by observing certain features of the heart rhythm
- The goal is to learn how to keep our ANS in balance by maintaining a calm, centered emotional state.
- This can be achieved through different means
- Slowing our breathing down and maintaining a steady breathing in and out breath rhythm helps stabilize the ANS
- Feelings of appreciation, love, caring, and other very positive emotions also help us to maintain a stabilized ANS
- With practice, you will be able to maintain a steady breathing and positive emotional state
- This practice will help modify your mind-body in such a way as to create new, healthier mental health patterns

First Session Practice

There are varying amounts of time that can be structured for client practices. For the first session, you will want to keep the session fairly short, or do a couple of short sessions interspersed with discussion or other techniques. For example, I would keep the actual training at no more than 20 minutes initially, or break it up into 10 minute time periods for the first session.

The main goal of the first session is to just orient the client to the HRV instrument, its features, what it does, and the goal. Use very simple and concrete terms with the client. It is recommended that you brainstorm how you might explain HRV with each client prior to actual training so you are not stumbling around trying to find the right way to say something.

Continued Session Practices

An overriding approach is to keep everything positive and fun. Praise any kind of effort and particularly praise any approximation they make in their progress. Be patient with the training to assure some kind of success on the client's part. For example, regardless of the progress, look for any percentage gain in either the moderate or high levels.

Be aware of cognitive fatigue, boredom, and frustration—all of which will cause negative responses. Although a client may tolerate longer training sessions, be careful; it is better to go slowly than to overdo it and trigger one of these negative responses.

You will find that each client will respond quite differently to the training. Your task is to accurately assess their responses, as well as have an idea ahead of time as to how you will respond. For example, how would you handle cognitive fatigue? Boredom? Frustration? Since these are three common responses, plan ahead on what you would do.

Session notes on your part are very important. This is where you write down anything that will help guide you in your training with each client. For example, make sure that you cover the following:
- Feelings, thoughts before and after each practice
- Sensations and other experiences during practice
- What they did that they believed helped them progress
- The suggestions you will make concerning transfer strategies
- Getting clear on why they may be struggling and then giving suggestions that may help
- Explaining goals for future sessions or for the training as a whole
- Home/in-class practice suggestions

Suggestions for Enhancing Training Effects

The training suggestions included in the company's protocols are a good starting point, but will surely be insufficient for all clients. Therefore, you will need a large repertoire of ideas and suggestions available as needed.

Begin with the standard protocols and follow the suggestions mentioned earlier. First, try and get a handle of the kinds of feedback that the client seems to prefer. Keep this in mind as you proceed forward. For example, as mentioned, try different modalities with different visual and auditory feedback and determine what they like, or what seems to work best for them.

There are two guidelines here: One is being sensitive to what they like or don't like and compensating as needed. The second is related to what additional protocols will enhance training effects.

Breath training

Because breathing patterns are extremely sensitive to stress and will display unique stress patterns from person to person, one cannot expect quick changes in this area. Breath training, while exceedingly important, can be very difficult to change and often triggers anxiety. By understanding this, consider breathing and breathing patterns from different points of view so that you can be as helpful as possible.

Although the training protocols emphasize breathing into the heart region, you also want to make sure that the client practices correct breathing. In fact, the client will likely progress more quickly with the training if they are practicing breathing correctly.

There are three core components of effective breathing: The volume of breath, rate, and rhythmic patterns of inhalation/exhalation over time. To help in attaining correct and efficient breathing, we teach clients diaphragmatic breathing, which emphasizes the use of the diaphragm; three-stage breathing, which emphasizes correct use of the diaphragm, lungs, and clavical region; slowing the rate of breathing; and improving steady patterns of breathing over time.

For example, it is helpful to use protocols that set a particular rate of breathing and then practice slowing the breathing down, while breathing in and out in a steady rhythmic pattern. Practice this for several minutes at a time.

Another approach you can take is to just have the client follow their breath as it comes in and out without attempting to make any changes. This tends to cause the least amount of stress and reduces excessive effort. Once they are comfortable with this, which may take a few sessions, then proceed gently with breathing rhythmically, or with diaphragmatic breathing. There are a number of ways to help encourage this form of breathing, but won't be covered here.

Once they seem relaxed with focusing on their breathing, proceed with having them focus on the heart region. I would still have them feel the breathing going down into the diaphragm, even though their focus is primarily in the heart region. This encourages correct breathing and also reduces the potential anxiety of focusing too much on the heart early on. However, seek assistance if anxiety continues to be an issue.

Open Focus Training

Although you are probably unfamiliar with the technique, Open Focus (Fehmi & Fritz, 1980) is an excellent relaxation/meditation technique and, for some, can work quite rapidly in inducing a calm inner state. A training tape and scripts are available; I would highly recommend trying it on your self because I am confident that you will find it to be a powerful tool.

Besides the suggestions mentioned here, there are many, many other suggestions that can be given to you. As you learn more about HRVB and practice with your clients, as well practice on your self, you will expand the above suggestions by adding more of your own. This is desirable because it will demonstrate increased knowledge on your part of HRVB and related training goals, as well as give you a lot more flexibility in individualizing your treatment strategies.

Other strategies that have already been discussed may greatly enhance HRVB training:

> The Six Second Quieting Response (QR)
>
> Autogenic Training Phrases (AT)
>
> Progressive Relaxation (PR)
>
> Use of Therapeutic Imagery

Generalization and Transfer of Skills into Daily Living Situations

Training your client to master the HRVB is only helpful if they are able to generalize these skills into daily living situations. Focus on skill transfer as soon as possible by making helpful suggestions and asking for feedback on how they are incorporating skills into different situations. Here are a few suggestions to get you started on teaching transfer skills:

- Educate the client on the HRVB process. They will have trouble being motivated if they cannot get their mind around what its all about
- Next, educate the client on the short-term goals, as well as how these goals correspond to his/her personal goals for change
- In every session that follows, review the goals, focusing in on the short-term goals in terms of actual progress
- Short-term goals could include any number of tasks. For example:

  -Ways they can remind themselves to think about the training and goals during the day

  -Positive changes, no matter how seemingly minor or subtle that seems to be tied to training.

  -Helpful reminders: A sticker or colored dot on personal property, a watch face, notebook, etc. The counselor may attach a sign or other indicator on the wall to remind clients. When a client is doing the training, the counselor can point to the sign as a friendly reminder. Seek assistance for constructing such reminders

  -Practice CDs that a client can take home and practice. You may also have them fill out some kind of check list or other way of documenting effects of practice

- Once the client gets to the point in the training where they seem to be mastering one of the four training levels, have them demonstrate transfer of skills. For example:

  -Turn the client away from the screen, turn the audio down and have them tell you when the levels rise and fall and to what extent. Make sure they are clearly tying what is happening experientially inside with the HRVB readings.

  -Either discuss with the client, or have the client imagine or think of common stressful situations while maintaining coherence.

  -At home: review situations that arise and check how they responded.

  -Do not move to the next level of difficulty until they can clearly demonstrate improvements in each of these areas.

8

Teaching Beginning Meditation: Enhanced Concentration Training

The Purpose of this Chapter

Understanding meditation from the standpoint of concentration

The role of the sensory-perceptual system and concentration

Strategies for enhancing concentration

Beginning Meditation

What is meditation? There exists a large array of definitions. Some refer to it as a kind of mental effort. Others believe it represents a particular state of consciousness. From my own position, I see both views to be relevant; that is, we can differentiate between the doing of meditation, which requires mental effort, and the state of consciousness that results from the mental effort. Besides different definitions, there are also a large array of meditation and related contemplative strategies. What all of these different meditative practices have in common, however, is that they all start with enhanced concentration training, which is the mental effort aspect of meditation. Becoming skilled in meditation is simply not possible without high level concentration skills. Occasionally a client will already possess strong concentration skills; therefore, they will move quickly through these strategies and be ready for more advanced meditation training.

One way to explain the depth of concentration that is needed is with an analogy. The intensity of concentration that is needed for deep meditation is similar to the intensity of concentration that an olympic athlete needs to perform well. This means that for those who want to achieve progress in their quest for meditative experience, we need to recognize that we will need to deepen our concentration skills. But, understand that enhanced concentration is not only necessary for meditation, but is also extremely helpful for practically anything you do in life, whether it is learning something new, increasing our memory, problem solving, controlling our negative emotions, practicing a sport, or any other important goal.

There are many excellent concentration strategies that can be taught but, unfortunately, it is not a simple manner in deciding which ones to use with which client. Each technique has its own unique effects and each client has his or her own unique needs (which also varies over time). It would not be prudent to present this complex issue in great detail now, but I will present a few key ideas that hopefully will guide you in developing an individual program with clients.

One way to understand concentration strategies is in the sensory-perceptual modality: either visual, auditory, kinesthetic, or a combination. This also corresponds to whether a technique might be considered more body oriented or more mental. For example, concentration on breathing is initially more kinesthetic and more body oriented, whereas repetition of a *mantra* (sound pattern) is initially more mental (although the goal of *mantra* is to stimulate emotional states as well). There is some validation for this view in the literature, where is has been shown that Transcendental Meditation (repeating a *mantra*) is more effective for reducing anxiety than, say, Progressive Relaxation (a more physical technique).

Another way to understand concentration techniques is in first understanding how the mind actively concentrates. The mind concentrates by taking an image, thought, etc,. and holds it for a brief period. Then it leaves it and takes another image, thought, etc., one after another. By understanding this, we can strengthen concentration by continually taking the same image, thought, etc., over and over at successive intervals. By requiring the mind to do this, the image, thought, etc., becomes intensified, which strengthens one of the dimensions of concentration/attention. And second, because we are controlling the image, thought, etc., we are strengthening yet another dimension of concentration.

One very common concentration technique that uses this approach is in the practice of *mantra*. We repeat the sound pattern with brief intervals of space between each sound repetition. Holding the mind forcefully on something for very long can create strain, but if we hold it briefly, let it go, then bring it back, we do not cause strain.

Besides an auditory concentration technique, this can also be applied with variation to visual concentration techniques, such a concentrating on a flower. Rather than looking at only one part of the flower, which can cause eye strain, it is better to shift the eyes just slightly at regular intervals. This allows the mind to accept images that are just slightly different but still very much related to the overall image of the flower without creating strain.

Another variation on this would be to visually concentrate on the same flower for 8 to 12 seconds, close the eyes and then visualize the after-image for 8 to 12 seconds. This also helps prevent strain.

I have found that strain seems to be much more of a problem with visual concentration than with auditory or kinesthetic concentration, so be very aware of this tendency when working with clients. Clients who come to therapy probably already have a problem of visual strain from current concentration difficulties and an over use of the visual sense. From reading, driving, computers, T.V., etc., our culture overemphasizes the visual realm, so the eyes are often tired and strained. By being aware of this, you can teach them the proper way to visually concentrate, as well as encouraging them to use more auditory or kinesthetic concentration when possible to reduce tension.

Points to Remember and Emphasize with Clients:

There are visual, auditory, and kinesthetic concentration strategies, as well as various combinations of these.

Some strategies work better for certain types of problems (or for certain types of growth processes).

The mind actively concentrates by taking an idea, image, thought, or sensation and holds it briefly, then lets it go. If you try to hold the mind too long on something, it causes strain.

By learning to direct and hold the mind in the proper manner, you can strengthen your concentration abilities without causing strain.

With these points in mind, let us now consider some techniques that can be used in assisting your clients in strengthening their concentration

Counting the Breath

This is a kinesthetic concentration technique that fits well with the other training procedures. It can also be added to the breathing exercises that you have already prescribed. Not only is this a concentration technique, but if done correctly, it has the additional benefit of normalizing incorrect breathing patterns, as well as teaching a correct posture for sitting and proper breathing.

Rather than simply observing the breathing, which is extremely difficult for the beginner, we start by counting the inhalation and exhalation. Counting gives the mind something to hold onto so it doesn't wander.

I have found that the most significant procedure related to this technique is maintaining the correct sitting posture. Specifically, the spine needs to be kept properly aligned; meaning that it is straight (proper curvature), with the center of gravity in the very center of the body. To do this, sit on a firm chair, with the feet flat on the floor. The base of your pelvis should be planted firmly on the chair so that there is no sagging of the lumbar region. Make sure your chin is slightly tucked in. Imagine a string attached to the top of your head and lifting you slightly upward. Now rock forward and back on the pelvis, allowing the body to come to rest at it's balance point, where the pull of gravity is at a minimum. Now rock side to side, again allowing the body to come to rest at a point of balance. With practice, this is achieved quickly and easily. Next, rest your hands in your lap with the palms facing upward, your left hand resting on your right hand (this encourages greater relaxation).

Level One Training:

Now bring your awareness to your breathing. Note if you are naturally breathing in the three-stage manner described in the previous procedures on respiration. If not, do not attempt to change (this will distract you), but simply be aware of this goal in your imagination. As you practice observing the breath, and if you are maintaining the correct posture, correct breathing will come in time. Finally, have your eyes partially open, with your gaze directed somewhat downward; do not look at anything, just be aware of your visual field as a whole. You may also keep your eyes closed if you prefer. Try each way and do what is more comfortable. Now you are ready to count your breathing.

Begin by bringing your attention to your breathing. Now, as you begin to inhale, start counting a slow "o..n..e.." in your mind as you feel your abdomen and chest expanding. Then as begin to exhale, count a slow "t..w..o.." in your mind, as you feel your chest and abdomen contract. Continue this count until you reach 10. This is one round. If your mind wanders at all during the counting, start over with "one." When you have completed one round, start with "one" again and count to ten. Start with 6 minutes. When you can complete six minutes without losing your concentration, increase to 12 minutes. Do not be concerned if you have trouble concentrating in the beginning; after all, this is why you are doing the practice. Avoid emotionally reacting to the mind wandering; just bring it back and start again with the round.

When you are able to sit for 20 to 30 minutes without losing your concentration, you will have attained good concentration and should notice a dramatic increase in your awareness of subtle changes in your body and mind. Even though this is an active concentration technique, you will also notice that your passive concentration skills are also increasing.

If your clients want advanced training in this technique, have them extend the counting to 30 to 45 minutes at a time without losing concentration.

Level Two Training:

After a few months of the above practice a client may wish to strengthen their concentration skills even further. Level Two also involves observing the breathing process. The difference is that instead of counting the breath, the client simply observes and follows the breath as it moves in and out. Start with an approximate three minute session in the beginning. Again, if your mind wanders during this time, simply bring it back and start over. When you are able to do three minutes without your mind wandering, increase to six minutes, and then to nine, etc.

This is a very difficult concentration exercise. While it may not seem that it would be that much more difficult than counting the breath, the counting really helps to control the mind. Without counting, what we focus on—the breathing—is far more subtle and, therefore, significantly more difficult to attend to. In the beginning you will likely find that even three minutes requires a lot of mental effort.

If your client is able to reach 20 to 30 minutes, they will have attained a very high level of concentration ability and will be able to slip in and out of passive concentration with little difficulty This level of concentration is seldom found in the vast majority of individuals, so it offers significant benefits.

Mantra Concentration

The use of a *mantra* or sound pattern was popularized in the West by Transcendental Meditation. *Mantra* has been a widely used method of concentration in the East for centuries; and in Tantra yoga, there is a very elaborate body of knowledge on the psychophysio-spiritual effects of sound.

Mantra is obviously an auditory concentration technique. It is a very effective and fairly easy way to hold the mind's attention and prevent it from wandering or obsessing on certain thoughts. It is very difficult to repeat a *mantra* and think of anything else. Try it right now and you will see what I mean. This is why research has shown that the repetition of *mantra* is very effective for anxiety; it is very good for stopping negative, worrisome thoughts.

Let me add that when repeating a *mantra*, one is not inhibiting or suppressing anything; rather, one is simply choosing where they wish their mind to be and have the ability to keep it there. This, in turn, helps break negative thought patterns that have become habitual. This also does not mean that there is no need to address negative issues; that is not the role of *mantra*, whose role is more cognitive behavioral. Just because you are addressing an issue doesn't mean you still won't continually fall into its habit. The power of concentration techniques like mantra is to help break these habit patterns.

If we look at the science of *mantra* as taught in Tantra yoga, we find that it is actually quite complex. *Mantras* are believed to be sound patterns that have very specific mind-body effects and, therefore, should be used according to a person's make-up and specific needs. While I would concur with this view, unfortunately, it is impossible to teach *mantra* as such within this context. Fortunately, however, there are also "general" *mantras* that are not overly specific and are considered to be effective for most people. Examples of these are: Rama (pronounced "rahma"), Hil (pronounced "hill"), Om (pronounced "ah-oh-mm"), Hum (pronounced "humm"), Hu (pronounced "hugh"). You also can use simple words like "one" or "relax" if you prefer, although they are not considered really *mantras* and do not have the same kind of mind-body effects. However, they can still benefit a person in at least certain ways that are similar to *mantras*. Try out these different sounds presented here and pick the one in which you feel most comfortable.

You are now ready to begin the practice. Sit comfortably in a firm chair so that the spine is fairly straight, or you can use the sitting position described in "Counting the Breath" exercise. Bring your awareness to your *mantra* and begin repeating it, first out loud. The faster and louder you repeat it, the easier it is to hold your concentration, so play around with it until you find the volume and speed that works and feels right (this will also vary some from practice to practice).

When you say the *mantra*, make sure that there is a brief pause or void between the saying of the *mantra* and before you say it again. Adjust the saying of the *mantra* so that it takes approximately the same amount of time for the pause as it takes to say the *mantra*. The actual speed that you say the *mantra* will not affect this timing. A little practice with this and you will find that it becomes relatively easy to accomplish and soon becomes natural. The purpose of the pause or void is to allow the mind to relax and to passively attend to the task. This prevents stress or strain on the system, as well as teaching one how to passively concentrate on the mind-body affects.

Start with an approximate 10 minute practice. After 2 to 4 weeks of daily practice, you can increase to 20 minutes if you would like.

Once you get used to saying your *mantra* out loud and maintaining your concentration, you can begin to practice saying it within yourself during the 10-20 minute practice time. At this point, you can also begin to practice at other times, such as at work or when working around the house.

Eventually, you want the *mantra* to become habitual to the point where the unconscious is continually bringing it up to the conscious level during the day. At this point it starts becoming second nature to you. I tend to think of my *mantra* as a good friend who is always right here now to keep my mind alert and positive. You will find the *mantra* becoming stronger with practice; in other words, more effective in concentrating your mind, calming your body, and stopping negative thoughts and images.

To enhance the concentration and relaxation affects, you can add a kinesthetic component to your *mantra*. When you say the *mantra* out loud, you can concentrate on your body and feel the vibration of the *mantric* sound. The tone and pitch will vary from *mantra* to *mantra* and also according to how you say the *mantra*, and this will cause different vibratory effects on your body. Just allow yourself to experience these effects as you practice. Feeling the *mantra* kinesthetically will draw you more into the experience of the *mantra* and you will find that it can be very soothing and calming on your body and can help stimulate certain pleasant emotions. For example, I have found that the *mantra* "Rama," when said at the right pitch and with full concentration, can vibrate the abdomen and chest/heart regions. Emotionally, it can stimulate strong feelings of love and joy. This may seem hard to believe, but that has been my experience (as well as for others). I have been able to shift from feelings of sadness, frustration, or anger to joy within seconds using this *mantra*.

Mantras are powerful initiators of psychophysiological change. While some may feel that such effects are more from suggestion or auto-suggestion than anything else, only research will be able to validate or invalidate this. In the meantime, it really doesn't matter as long as they create the kind of experiences that you want.

You can also increase your passive concentration skills by pausing longer between the intervals of saying the *mantra*. Attend only to the Void and just experience it without thought or emotional reaction. Extending the pause via passive concentration gets easier with practice. You will find that if you can extend the Void for more than several seconds, it also brings a very peaceful feeling that is difficult to describe; it must be experienced to appreciate. In Zen and other teachings, it is often described as "sitting, doing nothing." What this means is that one has shifted their consciousness in such a way that habitual thoughts, feelings, etc., do not arise in the mind. I have found that in such a state many creative insights and intuitions arise spontaneously. If such experiences cause you to start thinking about them, the spontaneous process is stopped and you shift back into a more habitual state. In other words, the Void is a here and now experience; if you react to it, you are taken out of the here and now and, consequently, you lose it. All this may sound somewhat abstract and vague to you, but once you experience it, it becomes quite clear.

Circle Concentration

This is a very simple and brief, but very powerful concentration training technique. I have used it myself with excellent results.

Take a sheet of white paper and draw an approximately one inch circle in the center of the paper. You can use a nickel which, after drawing the circle, will be close to one inch. Use a thin black marker to give you a very definitive circle. Attach the paper at eye level approximately eleven and a half inches from your eyes. Make sure that it is dark enough behind the paper that light or shadow does not come through.

Important: Keep shifting your eyes slightly to various areas of the circle in slow, easy, short (1/4"-1/2") movements. Do not stare at any one area for more than a few seconds. If your mind wanders during this time, start again. If you find that 30 seconds is too long, reduce it to 15 seconds.

When you are able to hold your mind on the circle for 30 seconds, increase to 60 seconds, then to 90 seconds, then two minutes, then two and a half minutes, and finally to three minutes without losing your concentration.

Within 3 to 4 weeks, you should begin to notice an improvement. This will continue to strengthen as you practice. Don't be fooled by the brevity of this technique; you will find that it is not easy to control your thoughts for three minutes at a time. The ability to do so demonstrates very good concentration.

A variation of this technique, and one that further reduces the likelihood of eye strain, is to look at the circle for 10 to 12 seconds and then close your eyes and observe the after image for 10 to 12 seconds or until it fades, whichever occurs first. This constitutes one round. Build to 10 to 20 rounds without having your mind wander.

For some reason, I have found the technique to be particularly helpful for strengthening one's rational or cognitive capacities; in other words, the ability to think through and understand something in a logical and rational manner. How this is achieved, I'm not sure, but it appears to relate to the visual aspects of the technique and, of course, the ability to hold the mind on particular thoughts.

While there are many people who are quite rational and may even overly rely on logic, there are also many people who are quite weak in there use of rational thinking They may be in school or work settings where strong logic is needed to a greater degree. Such people will often experience strain because of their weakness, stressing themselves in an attempt to control their minds. I might add that we also live in a society that over emphasizes this skill and, consequently, we must adapt to this challenge effectively.

One of the enticements of this technique is in its simplicity and brevity. It takes very little time and yet can provide outstanding benefits. All you need to do is just look at the circle. You can look inside the circle, at the black ring, or around the outside of the circle. Study it, watch it, let it do its thing (i.e., double images, colors, lights, movements, etc.; such visuals actually demonstrate that you are concentrating effectively). Blink when necessary.

About the Appendixes

Appendix A

Imagery Enhancement Training. This is a script for teaching your clients IET. Once you learn the script, feel free to individualize it as you see fit your each client. Record the script on a CD and recommend that the client practice at least once a day. Continue the practice at least two to three weeks, or until you are confident that the client has improved his or her imagery skills. You can also return to it whenever you feel it is needed. In addition, some clients who struggle with insomnia find that the CD is very helpful.

Appendix B

Integrated Relaxation. As the name implies, this is a general relaxation sequence for your clients. The technique is really just an integration of three relaxation techniques: Autogenic, Progressive Relaxation, and therapeutic imagery. I often use this during workshops and in-services, or when I am only conducting a very limited numbers of treatment sessions. It also works well for maintenance practice.

Appendix C

Home Training Cards. These can be copied on card stock or laminated for the client to take home. They are a quick reminder of some of the steps for three very important techniques: Diaphragmatic breathing, Progressive Relaxation, and Alert Mind-Calm Body techniques. The cards are small enough to be carried in a shirt pocket or purse for quick practices during the day.

Appendix D

Home Practice Diary. It is very important that the client practice various exercises, techniques, and strategies between sessions. This, of course, is critical for real change, as well as for generalization. Included are a couple that I developed. Feel free to create your own using these as a guide.

Appendix E

Session Notes. You may already have a way of structuring your clinical notes. What I have included is simply ways to keep track of important points with your clients as related to teaching the strategies in this book.

Appendix A

Imagery Enhancement Training Script

This imagery transcript is derived from three sources: Weitzman's Imagery, Fehmi's Open Focus training, and my own contributions.

After sitting comfortably, close your eyes, and make sure that your body is in a relaxed position...with your arms at your sides or in your lap but not touching your sides, palms facing upward...and your legs uncrossed

As your listen to my voice, allow your breathing to move down from the chest and into the abdomen...gently let the abdomen rise and fall with each breath...regularly, rhythmically, effortlessly...from the top of your head to the tip of your toes, allow all of the tension to flow out of your body...forehead becoming smooth and cool...eyes, and the muscles around your eyes becoming heavy and relaxed...facial muscles becoming relaxed...and the jaw becoming loose and limp...

Allow your neck and shoulder muscles to become loose and limp...allowing heaviness and warmth to flow downward from your shoulders into your arms, legs, and entire body...

Allow your mind to gently concentrate on this exercise, allowing all other thoughts to be put aside for the time being...remember...this is your time...make the best use of it...by allowing yourself to just be here right now...

This technique will concern itself with Imagery Enhancement Training. This is the ability to self-regulate your images...that is...you will learn to gently concentrate your mind on particular images...and you will practice encouraging these images to be as vivid and as real as possible.

You will also learn to change the images at will. This training will help you in further developing your self-regulation skills.

I will be presenting certain images for you to image for approximately 15 seconds... some of these images are visual, and you will be asked to see them in your mind...others are auditory, and you will be asked to hear them in your mind...and still others are feeling images, and you will be asked to feel them.

When an image is presented, just allow yourself to experience the image as it is presented, allowing it to be experienced as vividly and real as possible. Once you are experiencing the image for the 15 seconds, I will be asking you to either hold the image gently as it is, or to change the image in some particular way...this will become more clear to you as we go along.

It is very important that you do not strain at all during this exercise. If you cannot produce the image, just relax and wait for the next image. Remember that you will not be able to produce all the images equally well...and that is O.K.

Just note in your mind any image that was difficult for you. Remember always to use your concentration through gentle persistence only...very little effort should be used...this gentle effort is only with the mind...the body is kept relaxed and not really involved.

Now...let us begin...

Wait 15 seconds between each question

Can you imagine the orange glow of a setting sun on the horizon?

Can you gently hold this image in your mind's eye a little longer?

Can you imagine the sound of the wind blowing through the trees?

Can you gently hold this image, listening intensely to this sound?

Can you imagine a single flower-a daisy-suspended in space in front of you?

Can you imagine the daisy changing and becoming a field of daisies?

Can you feel a sense of heaviness in the muscles of your arms?

Can you allow the heaviness to include your legs?

Is it possible for you to imagine the distance between your arms?

Can you continue to hold this image for a little while?

Can you see the color green in your mind?

Can you see the green color changing into the color blue?

Is it possible for you to feel a sense of sadness?

Can you now change this sadness to a feeling of happiness?

Can you imagine the smell of a cool spring morning?

Can you now imagine the smell of a warm summer day?

Is it possible for you to hear the sound of seagulls in the distance?

Can you continue to hear the seagulls for a little while?

I wonder if you can imagine the space inside your throat?

Can you allow this space to fill your chest as well?

Can you allow yourself to feel peaceful right now?

Can you hold this feeling gently and continue to enjoy it?

Is it possible for you to feel warmth in your body?

Can you feel this warmth while also feeling your forehead as cool?

I wonder if you can imagine the movement of water in a mountain stream?

Is it possible for you to imagine this water flowing over a waterfall?

Can you imagine the thickness of your legs?

Can you gently hold this image for a little while?

I wonder if you can sense a feeling of love and joy in your heart region right now?

Can you gently hold this feeling for a little while?

Is it possible for you to imagine sitting in a large bright yellow square?

Can you allow this square to grow larger and larger until it is as far as you can see?

Can you imagine your body feeling light and floating as if on a cloud?

Can you gently hold this feeling for a little while?

I wonder if you can imagine the sound of bells ringing in the distance?

Can you allow these bells to come closer and louder?

Is it possible for you to imagine the space around your body?

Can you imagine this space growing larger?

I wonder if you can feel a sense of inner acceptance of yourself just as you are?

Can you hold this contended feeling for a little while?

Can you see a large tree in your mind full of green leaves?

Can you imagine white buds among the green leaves?

I wonder if you imagine the taste of a fresh orange as you bite into it?

Can you change the taste by biting into a lemon?

Is it possible for you feel a tingling sensation in your fingers?

Can you also feel the tingling in your toes?

Can you imagine feeling anger right now?

Can you now let the anger go into a feeling of assertiveness and determination?

Can you imagine a feeling of discomfort in your abdomen?

Is it possible for you to feel the discomfort evaporating into a relaxed rippling of laughter and joy?

I wonder if you can imagine feeling confident in your ability to image vividly?

Can you gently hold this feeling for a little while?

As you continue to practice this exercise every day, you will find yourself developing your ability to image more and more vividly... as well as being able to change your images at will...

This ability becomes more and more easy and subtle... taking less and less effort... You learn to allow your mind to image at will... This ability will give you more control over your thoughts and feelings... allowing you to direct your mind where you wish to be...

Remember, either we are in control of our mind or our mind is in control of us. Through Imagery Enhancement Training, you are learning to take charge of your mind, and therefore of your life... This is always a gentle process...never forcing...just encouraging... What I call gentle persistence...

And now you may very gradually bring yourself out of this state of relaxation and imagery in the usual three steps...taking two deep breaths...stretching your arms, legs, and entire body...and slowing opening your eyes...feeling refreshed and relaxed...returning to your daily activities in an easy, gentle manner.

Appendix B

General Relaxation Instructions

** The number in parenthesis is the number of seconds that you pause **

Close your eyes...(3) and make sure that your body is in a comfortable position, with your arms resting in your lap or by your side...(5)

Just listen to my voice...(3) and as you listen to my voice, just let your mind focus on what I am saying. Let go of all other thoughts of things that have to be done, or things that should have been done, let all other thoughts go out of your mind, and make this your time...(3), time to yourself, just for yourself...(7)

Now...please bring your attention to your body...(5)

First bring your awareness to your breathing...(5)

Take a deep breath and hold it...(5) and then slowly let the breath go out...(3), feeling the breathing letting go as it leaves your body...(5)

Take another deep breath and hold it...(5), then again slowly let the breath go...(3), allowing the breathing to slowly go out...(5)

And one more time, take a deep breath and hold it (5), and again slowly letting the breath go...(3), allowing the breathing to slowly go out...(5)

Now bring your awareness to your entire body...(3)...and feel your body's weight against the chair...(5)

Feel where your body touches the chair...(3), and allow your body to feel heavy against the chair...(5)...Imagine your body becoming heavier and heavier against the chair...(5)

And as your body becomes heavier, imagine the heaviness sinking down into the floor beneath you...(5)

Allow your body to just sink...(3) Feel the sinking motion...(5)

It feels so good to let go and allow your body to just sink down, becoming heavier and heavier and heavier against the chair...(5), feeling the heaviness like a heavy rag doll all over...(5), heavy and limp...(3), heavy and limp...(7)

Andnowbringyourawarenesstoyourarmsandhands…(3),letallotherthoughtsgoandjustfocusonyourarmsandhands…(3),justfeelthem…(5)

And now I would like you to make your hands into a fist…(3) and tighten your hands up very tightly, and tighten your forearms and upper arms…(5)

Just hold it…(3) and feel the tightness…(5), feel how uncomfortable it is…(3) and now slowly allow the tension to let go…(3), just feel the tension letting go…(3) and feel what the arms and hands feel like when they are more relaxed…(7)

And, again, tighten your hands up very tightly, and tighten your forearms and upper arms…(5) Just hold it…(3) and feel the tightness…(5), feel how uncomfortable it is…(3) and now slowly allow the tension to let go…(3), just feel the tension letting go…(3) and feel what the arms and hands feel like when they are more relaxed…(7)

Now, while focusing on your arms and hands, repeat the phrase to yourself, "My arms and hands are heavy and warm…"(3), "My arms and hands are heavy and warm…"(5), feeling a sense of heaviness and warmth flowing into your arms and hands…(5), "My arms and hands are heavy and warm…"(7)

And now bring your awareness to your legs and feet…(5)

Now tense up your feet and legs by pulling your toes toward you while tightening your legs…(5) Hold the tension…(3), tighter, tighter, feel the uncomfortable sensation of tightness…(3) Now let the tension go…(3), just let the tension drain out of your legs and feet…(5), just let the tension go…(7)

Now, while focusing on your legs and feet, repeat the phrase to yourself, "My legs and feet are heavy and warm…"(3), "My legs and feet are heavy and warm…"(5), feeling a sense of heaviness and warmth flowing into your legs and feet…(5), "My legs and feet are heavy and warm…"(7)

And now bring your awareness to your entire body, feeling an overall sense of heaviness and warmth…(5) Arms, legs, and entire body…(3), from the top of your head to the tips of your toes, feeling all of the tension draining out of your body…(7)

Now imagine yourself lying on the beach by the ocean…(5) Feel the soft sand beneath you…(3) and the warm sun on your skin…(5) Just imagine this in your mind…(3) Lying on the sand, listening to the ocean waves coming into shore and going out again…(5) The rhythmical, continuous sound of the waves. You can feel the warm sun and a small breeze blowing across you...(3) and occasionally you can hear a seagull off in the distance...(5) Listening to the sound of the ocean waves coming in and going out makes you feel as if your body is floating on the waves...(5)

Just let all other thoughts go from your mind...(3) Just be there by the ocean, allowing yourself to completely let go...(3) Do this for yourself...(5)

And as you imagine this calm scene in your mind and feel it in your body, say to yourself, "I am at peace..." (3) "I am at peace..." (5) Feeling so calm, so peaceful: "I am at peace..."(7) "I am at peace..."(10)

Appendix C

Relaxation Cards

Breathing for Relaxation
- Personal anchor for bringing awareness to body.
- Bring awareness to current breathing pattern.
- Shift attention to abdomen region—sense this region.
- Allow breath to flow naturally downward into this area.
- Do not force, let it happen naturally.
- Use imagery, balloon, etc., as needed to increase ability.
- Be aware of mind-body shift toward calmness.
- Continue breathing this way and stay aware of calm feelings.

Tense–Relax
- Personal anchor for bringing awareness to body.
- Bring attention to most common bracing areas.
- Now tense these muscle groups and hold as you breath in.
- As you breathe out, let go of all the tension and feel tension-draining away over next several seconds.
- Stay with feeling of relaxation in muscle groups before shifting to next group of muscles.

Alert Mind-Calm Body
- Personal anchor for bringing awareness to body.
- Be aware of particular stress or just do for practice.
- As you begin to inhale an easy, deep breath, say to yourself, "Alert Mind-Calm Body."
- As you begin to exhale, relax your jaw, tongue, and shoulders while feeling a wave of warmth and
- Heaviness flowing down from your shoulders through your body and out your toes.
- Repeat as many times as necessary until you feel alert and calm.

Appendix D

Home Practice Diary

Date: _____
Today I practiced my:
    [ ] Stretching Exercises _____x;
    Areas of tightness: _____

    [ ] Breathing Exercises _____x
      ___**Diaphragmatic**
      ___**3-Stage** ___
      ___**Rhythm Breathing**
      ___**Other:**

    [ ] Relaxation Exercises _____x
      ___**Progressive**
      ___**Autogenic**
      ___**Imagery Enhancement Training**
      ___**Integrated Relaxation**
      ___**Other:**

Practice Experiences:

_____
_____

One joyful experience I had today was

_____
_____

Today I
    [ ] Grew and expanded
    [ ] Stayed the same
    [ ] Regressed

Appendix E

Clinical Notes

Client Name: _____ **Session#:** _____ **Date:** _____
Presenting Problem:

_____

Short Term Treatment Goals:

_____

Current Practice
Strategies:_____

Home Practice Review:
    [ ] **Frequency of practice:**
    [ ] **Feelings, thoughts before and after practice**
    [ ] **Sensations, experiences during practice**
    [ ] **Environmental conditions**
    [ ] **Generalization effects**

Home Practice Suggestions:

_____

_____

Biofeedback Modality: _____
Review of Session Training:

_____

_____

Goals for Home Practice and Next Session:

_____

_____

Notes:

_____

_____

Signature

References

Assagioli, R. (1961). *An introduction to psychosynthesis*. Psychosynthesis. Fifth International Congress of Psychotherapy, Vienna, Austria, August, 1961.

Assagioli, R. (1965). *Psychosynthesis: A manual of principles and techniques*. New York: Hobbs, Dorman.

Bandler, R. & Grinder, J. (1975). *Patterns of the hypnotic techniques of Milton H. Erickson, M.D.* Cupertire, CA: Merta Publications

Barrell, J., Aanastoos, C., Richards, A., & Arons, M. (1985). *Human science research methods*. Unpublished manuscript.

Berlyne, D. (1974). Perception. In E. Carterette, & M. Friedman(Eds.), *Handbook of perception: Volume one*. New York: Academic Press, (pp. 123-147).

Brown, B. (1977). *Stress and the art of biofeedback*. New York: Harper and Row.

Benson, H. (1975). *The relaxation response*. NY: William Morrow and Co.

Bhatnagar, S. (1980). *Innertuning: Synchronizing the self*. New York, NY: SRI International.

Black, S. (1969). *Mind and body*. London: William Kimber.

Brenna, S. (1972). *Yoga and medicine*. NY, NY: Penguin Group, Inc.

Davidson, J., & Goleman, D. (1977). The role of attention in meditation and hypnosis. *International Journal of Clinical and Experimental Hypnosis(4)*, 291-308.

Eliade, M. (1958). *Yoga: Immortality and freedom*. Princeton, NJ: Princeton University Press.

Fehmi, L., & Fritz, G. (1980). Open focus: The attentional Foundation of health and well-being. *Somatic*, Spring, 24-30.

Fischer, R. (1986). Toward a neuroscience of self-experience and states of self-awareness and interpreting interpretations. In B. Wolman & M. Ullman (Eds.). *Handbook of states of consciousness*. New York: Van Nostrand Reinhold,(pp. 3-30).

Fuller, G. (1980). *Behavioral medicine, stress management and biofeedback: A clinician's desk reference*. San Francisco, CA: Biofeedback Press.

Gaarder, K. (1979). Control of states of consciousness. In E. Peper, S. Ancoli, & Quinn (Eds.), *Mind/body integration*. New York: Plenum Press (pp. 47-56).

Green, E., Green, A., & Walters, E. (1979). Biofeedback for mind/body self-regulation: Healing and creativity. In E. Peper, S. Ancoli, & M. Quinn (Eds.), *Mind/body integration*. New York: Plenum Press.

Green, E., & Green, A. (1986). Biofeedback and states of consciousness. In B. Wolman & M. Ullman (Eds.), *Handbook of states of consciousness*. New York: Van Nostrand Reinhold (pp. 553-589).

Jacobson, E. (1934). *You must relax*. New York: McGraw-Hill.

Kapleau, P. (1965). *The three pillars of Zen*. Boston: Beacon Press.

Luthe, W. (1976). *Creativity mobilization technique.* New York: Grune and Stratton. Peper, E. (1976) Passive attention: The gateway to consciousness and autonomic control. In E. Peper, S. Ancoli, & M. Quinn (Eds.), <u>Mind/body integration</u>, New York: Plenum, (pp. 119-124)

Luthe, W. (1979). The methods of autogenic training. In E. Peper, S. Ancoli, & M. Quinn (Eds.), *Mind/body integration* New York: Plenum Press (pp. 167-186).

Peper, E. (1979). Passive attention: The gateway to consciousness and autonomic control. In E. Peper, S. Ancoli, & M. Quinn (Eds.), *Mind/body integration,* New York: Plenum (pp. 119-124).

Rolf, I. (1977). *Rolfing: Integration of human structures.* Santa Monica, CA: Landman Publishers.

Schwartz, G. (1981). Disregulation and systems theory. In D. Shapiro, J.

Stoyva, J. Kamiya, T. Barber, N. Miller, & G. Schwartz (Eds.), *Biofeedback and behavioral medicine.* New York: Aldine pp. 27-56).

Selye, H. (1956). *The stress of life.* New York: McGraw-Hill.

Schuman, M. (1980). The psychophysiological model of meditation and altered states of consciousness: A critical review. In J. Davidson, & R. Davidson (Eds.), *Psychobiology of Consciousness,* New York: Plenum, (pp. 349-374).

Schwartz, G. (1979). Biofeedback and physiological patterning in human emotion and consciousness. In E. Peper, S. Ancoli, & M. Quinn (Eds.), *Mind/Body Integration.* New York: Plenum Press (pp. 47-56). 57-68.

Singer, J. (1974). *Imagery and daydream methods in psychotherpay and behavior modification.* St. Louis: Academic Press.

Stroebel, C. (1979, September). Quieting response training. *Foundations of Biofeedback Practice: A Training Workshop for Professionals* (pp. 424-447). Philadelphia, PA: Biofeedback Society of America.

Vishnudevananda, S. (1959). *The complete illustrated book of yoga.* New York: Bell Publishing.

Wolpe, J. (1958). *Psychotherapy by reciprocal inhibition.* Palo Alto, CA: Stanford University Press.

About the Author

Dale Starcher has a doctorate in psychology and is a certified school psychologist. He has extensive training in the field of behavioral medicine, including stress management, biofeedback, therapeutic imagery, hypnotherapy, and body therapies. He also has a broad background in humanistic, existential, psychodynamic, and cognitive-behavioral treatment models, and has specialized in the treatment of childhood disorders, anxiety disorders, chronic pain, and traumatic brain injury. For the past 25 years he has also practiced, as well as taught, various yoga and zen practices. Dr. Starcher is an adjunct professor in the graduate school of education at Rider University.